# MARVIN A. ZUKER
# JUNE CALLWOOD

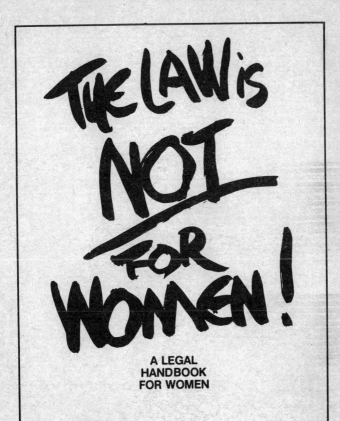

**A LEGAL
HANDBOOK
FOR WOMEN**

## Pitman Publishing

A division of Copp Clark Limited
Vancouver   Calgary   Toronto   Montreal

ISBN 0 273 04250 5

Pitman Publishing
517 Wellington Street West
Toronto  M5V 1G1
Printed and bound in Canada

# Introduction

It has been five years since we first took a real look at the legal rights and responsibilities of women in Canada. A great deal has been recommended since then, but very few changes have been implemented. International Women's Year has come and gone. It was a failure.

As we move into the second half of the seventies, we see that equality between men and women, and the notion that all people are equal under the law, are still only dreams.

Marriage and motherhood have become voluntary options rather than a manifest destiny for anyone born female. Yet for those who choose them, we still hear the same question being asked, **Do you work or are you a housewife?**

A wife's economic dependence on her husband has been considered one of the basic and most insidious factors contributing to the stress and strain of married life. Yet we still see the effects of financial coercion based upon individual behaviour or worthiness.

At a time when increasing efforts are being made to grant equal opportunities to all minority groups, we still see that there is one class of persons which deserves immediate attention—children—and in particular the blameless child—the illegitimate child. It is as though children are not considered people. Do they have any rights? How are they protected?

The future of Canada will be determined by the direction we now choose to take. If women are to be able to make full use of their capabilities, the change must come from all of society.

No book can ever replace professional consultation and advice. This book is primarily intended as a guide and it is an attempt to help make you aware. The rest is up to you.

Marvin A. Zuker    June Callwood

Toronto, Ontario
March, 1976

# Acknowledgments

Bob Beam, C.A., Professor of Accounting, Ryerson Polytechnical Institute, 50 Gould Street, Toronto, Ontario

Barbara Chisholm, Program Director, Canadian Council on Children and Youth, 1407 Yonge Street, Toronto, Ontario

Federation of Law Societies, Osgoode Hall, 130 Queen Street West, Toronto, Ontario

Mr. Ronald C. Merriam, Q.C., Executive Director, Canadian Bar Association, Suite 320, 90 Sparks Street, Ottawa, Ontario

Andrew M. Lawson, Provincial Director, Ontario Legal Aid Plan, Suite 1000, 145 King Street West, Toronto, Ontario

James E. Bennett and Pierre M. Loewe, Management Consultants, McKinsey & Company, Toronto, Ontario

Jane Lommel, Family Planning Federation of Canada, 88 Eglinton Avenue East, Room 404, Toronto, Ontario

Mr. K. P. Walsh, Estate Tax Officer, National Trust Company, 21 King Street East, Toronto, Ontario

Roger Schip, Photographer and Lecturer, Ryerson Polytechnical Institute, 50 Gould Street, Toronto, Ontario

# Contents

# 1  You are a child

If you are under the age of nineteen, you're a child in some of the provinces some of the time, and by a magic trick an adult the rest of the time. It will make life interesting for you, particularly if you leave home legally in one province and get picked up by the police in another for being under-age, or if you forget about provincial borders when ordering beer.

The Canadian Council on Children and Youth received a grant from the Secretary of State in 1974 to discover, among other matters, what *is* a child in Canada. It took a group of industrious researchers an entire summer to discover that we don't know.

You are too young to drink at eighteen in some provinces, and ready for a double in others. You commit a crime at the age of fifteen and you may be tried as a juvenile offender but, on the other hand, you may find yourself in an adult court. If your grandmother left you some bonds, you can have them when you are eighteen if you live in Manitoba, but inches away in Saskatchewan you'll have to wait another year.

If your parents are divorcing, the judge may ask you to make the ugly decision about which one you'll live with, providing you are twelve or more. If you're younger, the judge might talk it over with you but most of them don't. In either case, your wishes don't prevail, anyway.

Until you are eighteen or nineteen (depending on where you live in this disunified country), you are legally an "infant." You are not considered by the law to be capable of responsibility for yourself. The law therefore may not recognize any contract you have signed as binding; you cannot sue anyone or be sued directly; you may not be able to own land or write a will.

You can, however, drive a car, an expensive, complicated and potentially lethal piece of machinery. You can also become a parent at whatever age nature throws the switch, which can be as young as twelve. If you are female, you may keep the baby if you want to: the unlikelihood that you are knowledgeable or mature enough to care for the baby adequately will not be a factor.

Your name can be changed whether you like it or not. Your last name is your father's last name, unless your mother was never married to him. If a foster father turns up on the scene and the adults agree that he can adopt you, your last name becomes his. You can be taken from your parents and placed in a foster home in a strange city if that's what the court decides to do. Your parents or legal guardians have jurisdiction over your body: they can have your healthy kidney removed and donated to an ailing brother or sister without your approval.

It's obvious that children require protection. They don't have the experience or sufficient information to make life-changing decisions on their own. In fact, children deserve far more protection than they are now receiving in Canada against neglect, emotional deprivation, malnutrition and the caprice of parents, teachers, and social workers.

But the dilemma has been to decide at what age protection becomes stifling and an affliction. When, and in what areas, should autonomy begin? And until the child achieves the agreed-upon age of independence, is it good enough to leave her fate entirely in the hands of one or two parents who may or may not be competent, or even sane?

There has been considerable discussion in recent years about what is usually described as "the rights of children". Some feel that children should have an advocate whenever adults plan to do something drastic to them, such as deprive them of their freedom in the name of rehabilitation, or award custody of them to an agency or a divorced parent.

The advocate most commonly recommended is a lawyer, which seems reasonable since these crises occur in a courtroom setting. But it might be argued that there is nothing in legal training to equip lawyers to understand the emotional needs of children or to interpret their often confused and confusing behaviour.

In the meantime, Canadian children remain the most vulnerable of all citizens.

## Age of majority

Twenty-one is no longer the magic age. Canada had a wave of legislative change in the early Seventies which pushed back, along an uneven front, the age at which you become a legal adult.

The following is the age of majority in the various provinces and territories, together with the name and operative date of the pertinent statute:

*Nineteen* is the age of majority in British Columbia (Age of Majority Act 1970), New Brunswick (Age of Majority Act 1972), Newfoundland (The Minors [Attainment of Majority] Act 1971), Northwest Territories (Age of Majority Ordinance 1971), Nova Scotia (The Age of Majority Act 1971), and Yukon Territory (Age of Majority Ordinance 1972).

Eighteen is the age of majority in Alberta (The Age of Majority Act 1971), Manitoba (The Age of Majority Act 1970), Ontario (The Age of Majority and Accountability Act 1971), Prince Edward Island (The Age of Majority Act 1971), Quebec (Bill 66, an Act to Again Amend the Civil Code 1971), and Saskatchewan (The Age of Majority Act 1970).

## You and doctors

The attitude of doctors towards children derives from two elements, one practical and the other philosophical. The first is that children are moneyless, and not legally accountable for debts even if they have piggy banks. Therefore the doctor's fee depends upon the willingness of parents to assume the obligation, which depends in turn upon their consent to the doctor's administrations.

This in itself is not a sufficient reason for doctors to refuse to treat children without the expressed approval of parents or guardians. It probably never was, in the moral sense, but Canada's government-sponsored medical insurance is supposed to be universal and applies evenly to indigents, which is what children are.

The other concern is the operative one: the aspect of childhood imbedded in the law and custom which gives parents responsibility and jurisdiction over their children. In this sense, children are the property of parents. A doctor who gives treatment to a child without the knowledge and consent of the parents is risking legal action because she interfered with parental authority.

Doctors will hesitate to operate on you even in a life-threatening situation, such as if you are struck by a car and must have immediate brain surgery, until your parents can be located and give approval. As recently as a few years ago in Quebec, that approval had to come from a male parent; mothers were not considered competent to make the decision.

It is advisable, in fact, that when parents might be difficult to reach there should be a letter of consent to medical treatment left in a prominent place, such as pinned to your forehead, so as not to delay efforts to save your life in the event of an emergency.

It is understandable that doctors are reluctant to put themselves in legal jeopardy when faced with a child-patient who wants treatment in privacy. On the other hand, as they keep saying to one another at medical conventions, a child has as equal a right to medical care as any adult and perhaps as much claim to confidentiality.

Legal change to protect doctors against suit by indignant parents is under consideration because of the pressure of increasingly early puberty in today's healthier children. Since girls can menstruate as early as eleven, there are at least five possible years when their chronological age classifies them as children while at the same time they are physically mature.

During those adolescent years of emotional upheaval, crushes and longings, it is possible for you to have sexual relations which may result in a pregnancy or venereal disease, both of which demand a doctor's attention. If you have been concealing your sexual activities from your parents, as many young people do, and if you hope to continue to keep them in the dark, you will hope to find a doctor who won't tell. You very likely can't.

It is safer for the doctor to withhold treatment until your parents have been notified. In some localities, notably Vancouver and Toronto, doctors have made some adjustments to the stunning increase of teen-aged pregnancies, teen-agers asking for contraceptives and teen-agers with venereal disease. Both British Columbia and Ontario have lowered their age of consent for abortion, birth control and treatment for venereal disease from eighteen to sixteen. In practice, some doctors observe no age limit at all. In order to prevent pregnancies in girls as young as thirteen, the Hospital for Sick Children in Toronto, for instance, reluctantly and after considerable internal and psychological investigation, provides contraceptives for girls as young as thirteen.

Canadian doctors police themselves, and instances of unauthorized treatment of a minor rarely come to the attention of the general public. There was a case in British Columbia some years ago where a doctor inserted a contraceptive device in the uterus of a fifteen-year-old and was condemned by a subsequent medical inquiry. He appealed the ruling to the Supreme Court of British Columbia, which wanted no part of the controversy. The judge declared that doctors should make up their own minds how they felt about treating children.

There have been a number of celebrated cases in Canada where parents refused consent for medical procedures which doctors thought were necessary to save a child's life. This occurs most commonly when newborns of Rh-Negative mothers must have blood replacement to survive and the parents are members of the Jehovah's Witnesses, a sect which opposes blood transfusions. All provinces have legislation which provides for immediate custody hearings at any hour, based on child neglect provisions in the law, during which custody of the baby is transferred on a temporary basis to a child care agency, which approves the transfusion. The baby is returned to the custody of the parents after the transfusion but there is no record of how well the child flourishes emotionally, in view of the parents' conviction that something against God's law has been done.

There is federal legislation which states that Canadians over the age of sixteen and under the age of twenty-one can be treated by a qualified doctor or dentist without parental consent providing the professional in question has first made exhaustive attempts to locate the parents. This base line appears in most provincial legislation as well. The provinces differ, however, as to the age when parental involvement is unnecessary. As said, it is sixteen in Ontario and British Columbia, but in Newfoundland it is nineteen, and in other provinces and territories the age is eighteen.

If you wish to obtain birth control counselling, an abortion, medical care for a pregnancy, or treatment for venereal disease, without the knowledge of your parents, consult the women's centre nearest you. Public health nurses are sometimes helpful. In some places, the YWCA or YWHA will be sympathetic.

## You and school

In most provinces, attendance at school is compulsory for all children under the age of sixteen. If you fail to attend you are breaking the law; children have been sent to training school for truancy. If your parents keep you away from school, they can be arrested and fined.

You are excused from attending while ill or if you live a great distance from the nearest school and there is no transportation. In all provinces except British Columbia, Ontario, and New Brunswick, you can be excused from attending school for a short period if you are needed at home or for farm work.

The law forbids children under school-leaving age to take paid jobs during school hours. In Newfoundland, however, where school is compulsory only to the age of fifteen, a child younger than that can obtain a certificate and take a job. Prince Edward Island also has a school-leaving age of fifteen; PEI children younger than fifteen can work instead of attending school if there is poverty in the home, a regulation which could play havoc with the lives of the children whose families exercise it.

5   You are a child

Nova Scotia permits children as young as fourteen to leave school if they live outside the cities and towns; urban children must be sixteen.

New Brunswick children can leave school at fifteen, or earlier if they have passed Grade 12 at a precocious age, or if the Minister of Education agrees with the reasons for school-leaving advanced by the parents.

Quebec has compulsory school attendance until the age of fifteen. No child can work for more than six weeks in any school year and the work must be home or farm duties or caring for someone in the family.

Ontario sets the school-leaving age at sixteen, or whenever secondary schooling is completed— whichever comes first. The province does not normally allow work exemptions. However, early-leaving is becoming common: permission is granted to those young people, mainly disruptive males, who cause the administration distress.

Manitoba requires school attendance until the age of sixteen and allows work exemptions for not more than four weeks per year for home duties or caring for farm animals.

The age in Saskatchewan is sixteen but that province permits children younger than that to leave if they have finished Grade 8, and exempts children who work to support themselves or others, which can work an injustice on children of the poor.

Alberta has a school-leaving age of sixteen and grants exemptions of not more than three weeks per term for reasons of farming, home duties or maintaining self or others.

British Columbia permits school-leaving at fifteen except when the child has finished Grade 8 and there is no transportation to a high school.

In Newfoundland, Nova Scotia, Ontario, and Quebec, you must attend school until the end of the school year in which you become of age. In Manitoba you attend until the end of the term in which you have your sixteenth birthday. In most other provinces you can leave on your birthday, except in Alberta where you must complete the year if your birthday falls in the final term.

The country can sometimes be stern about school attendance, which was designed to rescue children from work exploitation and illiteracy, but incidents of enforcement have seemed somewhat arbitrary. Doukhobor children, for instance, literally were kidnapped from their homes because the government insisted on providing them with a non-Doukhobor education, but Indian children in northwestern Ontario had no schools for more than a decade. All over the country children are deprived of schooling whenever it is inconvenient or expensive to supply it, such as when children are handicapped, or in hospitals, or in detention centres or group homes.

Many thousands of children in Canada have learning disabilities or emotional problems which require intimate and expert teaching techniques. Since these methods are costly and poorly appreciated, only highly sophisticated urban school systems bother providing them, with the result that children who cannot make use of the standard technique of conveying information leave school illiterate, discouraged and bitter.

The Ontario Supreme Court ruled in 1975 that such a child, a fifteen-year-old Kitchener boy, must be subsidized by the provincial government which had failed to provide facilities to meet his learning problem, which was the common one of dyslexia. His mother was reimbursed the $12,000 it had cost her to place the child in a school in the United States which was prepared to deal with his handicap.

The success of this court action suggests that parents of children who are not receiving an education which takes into account their learning disability should sue the government. In 1974 the Maryland Association for Retarded Children sued the state government for failing to provide education programs for severely and profoundly retarded children. The court there ruled in favour of the Association and held that the lack of suitable education was a violation of the rights of those children. Such "class action" suits are not restricted in Canada but individual parents are free to sue, and should.

British Columbia's Berger Commission of 1975 recommended that one of the rights of children in that province should be "the right to an education which will ensure every child the opportunity to reach and exercise his or her full potential". It suggested that parents should be able to demand that the government maintain that right to a receivable education.

## Child labour

Children are everywhere allowed to work for no pay. Parents or any other adult in charge of the child are free to inflict punishment if the child refuses to provide free labour.

Oddly, when children are paid for the work they do, they automatically are protected from abuse. There are strict regulations concerning their health and safety and it is not permitted the employer to strike them.

7   You are a child

The Canada Labour (Standards) Code and Regulations doesn't establish an absolute minimum age for working children. It does, however, set down certain job conditions which must be observed whenever employees are younger than seventeen.

You can work for pay when you are younger than seventeen only if you are excused from school, only if the work is not likely to injure your health or endanger your safety, and only if you are not employed underground or in a prohibited job. The last refers to jobs covered by the Explosives Regulations, the Atomic Energy Regulations and the Canada Shipping Act.

Workers under seventeen are not allowed to do night shifts or to be on the job at any time after eleven at night or before six in the morning. There is a minimum wage for child labour which is significantly lower than the adult minimum wage, which accounts for the extensive and crippling use of children in stoop-labour occupations such as sugar beet farms. In 1972 the wage was a dollar an hour in federal jurisdictions, but provinces allowed even less. Alberta, for instance, permitted young girls to be paid fifty-five cents an hour.

It can be argued that low wages for children offer less enticement for leaving school. Employers are particularly keen on this reasoning, but the fact is that most child-employment takes place in the summer outside of school hours.

Dependent children are not required by law to give all their earnings to their parents, but parents are within their rights to demand it.

Income taxes are not selective as to age. Children who earn more than the amount established as a minimum for dependency must file an income tax and will no longer be classed as deductible on their parents' tax forms.

## Custody

If your parents are separating or planning a divorce, you will probably be assigned to your mother if you are (a) younger than seven, or (b) between seven and fourteen and female. Over the age of twelve (and sometimes earlier), the judge may consult with you concerning your preference but is not required to follow it.

Custody actions are tragic events for children. Court observers agree that most children love both parents and long for a reconciliation: to be asked to choose one, or to be awarded arbitrarily to one, is a no-win situation. Their misery is rendered more acute because in the majority of custody actions the parents are in a war of vengeance, in which the children figure as symbols of victory.

In the United States there are a handful of double-custody arrangements that have been approved by courts, in which the children live half of the time with one parent and half with the other. These appear to be rare, or maybe non-existent, in Canada as yet.

What is happening in this country is the development of two trends, one of which is to pay closer attention to the well-being of the children rather than to lump them in with the silver teapots as part of the property settlement.

Chief Justice Jules Deschenes of the Quebec Supreme Court commented in 1974, "It is high time we authorize the autonomous participation of children in these debates." The Berger Commission of British Columbia concurred, recommending that children should have "the right to independent adult counselling and legal assistance in relation to all decisions affecting guardianship, custody, or a determination of status."

The other trend is the growing number of fathers who are seeking and winning custody of children even without what was once the requisite of proving the mother unfit. The parental skills of men, who frequently are unabashed, full participants in infant care, are emerging as a factor in custody suits involving young children, which for many years were won automatically by women.

## You and law-breaking

In the late 1920s it was considered a progressive piece of legislation when Canada established juvenile courts where children who committed crimes would be examined in private hearings that protected their identity, and could then be given indeterminate sentences that allowed them to be released whenever their improved behaviour warranted it, rather than lingering past the moment of rehabilitation until the sentence had been served.

In practice it has worked against children. Social agencies and parents who simply couldn't abide a child made use of the courts to ship the young person away to a "training school". These children were often healthily obstreperous boys, sexually active girls, children disliked by their parents, or emotionally ill children. Not infrequently the well-intentioned indeterminate sentences turned out to be longer than adult courts would have imposed for the offense. When children were big and strong, training schools with adjoining farms tended to keep them until their birthdays took them out of the jurisdiction of juvenile courts.

9  You are a child

Training schools have been described as society's "miscellaneous file" or, more graphically, "the garbage heap of children". They also proved to be institutions where the most significant training was in crime and rebellion.

In 1975 the federal government climaxed a series of consultations with the provinces by issuing proposals for new legislation to replace the 1929 Juvenile Delinquents Act. The previous minimum age for juvenile delinquency charges was seven, which an enlightened society agrees is rather young for an arrest. The minimum age has been doubled to fourteen, the maximum has been set at eighteen years; young people in the age group between will have their offenses heard in what has been designated as a Youth Court if the provincial Attorney-General agrees that the trial should proceed. The Youth Court is provided with a battery of sophisticated diagnostic tools and sentencing alternatives, including restitution by the young person for whatever damage was done to the victim.

The Youth Court and the fourteen- to eighteen-year age range obtain only to offenses which fall under federal jurisdiction. It is expected that provinces gradually will adjust their own legislation accordingly, but in the meantime Saskatchewan, Ontario, New Brunswick, Nova Scotia, Prince Edward Island, the Yukon and the Northwest Territories establish the upper limit of juvenile delinquency at sixteen years of age; British Columbia sets the age at seventeen, and in Manitoba and Quebec the age is eighteen. In Alberta the age is sixteen for boys but eighteen for girls, an anachronistic control of the latter's sexuality, and in Newfoundland, which came into Confederation too late for the Juvenile Delinquents Act, the province decided the age should be seventeen.

The federal government published its proposals for the new legislation under the title *Youth and the Law*. It noted, "Any discussion involving youth and the law must consider that young persons in trouble are often children in need: children in need of parents, homes, education, understanding, supervision and respect."

It therefore suggests a bolstering of families whose children are disrupting the community, rather than the previous response which removed the child to a locked training school. As an alternative to creative efforts to help the family, it is expected that children in difficulty will be placed in family-like group home settings until such time as they can be independent or returned to their parents. It means for this age group a switch from police and corrections administration to child service agencies. Since the latter are provincial jurisdictions, *Youth and the Law* is understandably silent on this aspect of the proposals.

The aim of the new legislation is flexibility: young people who break the law may not even be charged with the offense if the circumstances warrant it, or the young person may be charged and convicted in Youth Court but not incarcerated, or the young person may be moved to adult court and suffer the full catastrophe.

If the young person does appear in court, lawyers will be provided for the defense.

Central Toronto Youth Services, a demonstration program funded by the Ontario government to meet the needs of difficult-to-reach children, recommended in June 1975 that children should have legal representation whenever they are in conflict with the law. It suggested a "law guardian" with access to psychiatrists, psychologists, social workers and other appropriate persons to help decide what is best for the child, with court funds available to obtain evidence from assessment services and schools, and that involuntary detention of children should happen only when it has been demonstrated that all other means have failed—such detention to be brief and subject to frequent review.

Judge George M. Thomson, a Family Court judge in Kingston, Ontario, recommended at a Montreal Rights of Children conference in 1973 that children caught in the legal process should be guaranteed a right to be heard. "Furthermore," he added, "I think we often forget that not only is the child entitled to be heard, he is also entitled to understand. Too many studies indicate that we fail to explain to the child what we are doing for or to him and why."

He picked up a phrase used by Milton Luger of the New York State Division for Youth: the child's "right to fail". Treatment and protection services for children, he explained, frequently expect a rapid change for the better in behaviour: children need to be permitted to fall below the therapist's expectations.

British Columbia's Berger Commission on Children's Rights had much to say about children who offend the law: the right to be consulted, for instance; the right to a competent interpreter where language or disability is a barrier to understanding; and the right to an explanation of all decisions affecting guardianship, custody or a determination of status.

A similar attitude was expressed in *Working Paper I The Family Court*, issued by the Law Reform Commission of Canada. It calls for "independent legal counsel" to represent the child, that person to have the same rights and privileges as the lawyers representing adults, and permission to use the court's investigative services.

The reasonableness of all these similar proposals gives some

11   You are a child

indication of the abuse of children in present juvenile courts.

## You and sex

If you are under the age of fourteen, anyone who has sexual relations with you can be given a life sentence. Boys under the age of fourteen, however, are excluded from this penalty.

If you are between the ages of fourteen and sixteen and you have sexual relations, your partner can be sent to prison for up to five years providing you had "a previously chaste character", which means that you were a virgin. Before deciding on the guilt of your partner, the court is going to ask a lot of questions about your behaviour so be prepared to defend yourself.

Women between sixteen and eighteen years of age also put their partners in jeopardy. Providing the women can prove they were "previously chaste" the partner can be sentenced for up to two years in prison.

The partner in all cases is specified as male only.

## Liability

The law leaves a vague area here. If it is determined by the court that you are old enough to distinguish right from wrong, you may be held accountable for whatever damage you do. Strictly speaking, however, until the age of majority your parents or a "next friend", who can be anyone the court recognizes, can sue on your behalf or represent you if you are sued.

If you win the suit the court will hold the loot until you come of age. Some adjustment can be made with the Trustee if you are in urgent need of the money. If you lose, you can be compelled to pay just as adults are. Your wages can be garnisheed and your property and bank accounts seized.

Contracts signed by you are usually voidable at your option alone until you reach the age of majority. If you are able to obtain credit for the necessities of life, such as food, rent and clothing, you are the responsible party.

The law is concerned that immature people are impulsive and can be gulled more readily than others. Therefore any document you sign except for those dealing with necessities can be challenged by you or the people you have contracted with. The other exception is a contract involving service or apprenticeship. "Infant" employees are often bound by their contracts of service with employers, so long as it can be shown that the contract was made for your benefit.

Unless you are in the armed forces you cannot make a will until you reach the age of majority. You cannot register documents but you can inherit, though you will not be permitted access to your inheritance.

People who are infants in the eyes of the law sometimes marry, which changes everything. An infant male, for instance, can give consent for his wife to have surgery: he becomes her parent. An infant wife is permitted to take legal action to protect her matrimonial rights. An infant wife is allowed to make a will.

## Your right to support

Your parents are obliged by law to provide you with food, clothing, medical attention and shelter, and the environment of the home must not threaten your health, sanity or morals. The latter refers mostly to parents who urge you into prostitution, use you for sexual relations themselves, or lead you into crime.

In return for this they are entitled a considerable amount of latitude in your upbringing. They can physically abuse and restrain you, providing it doesn't result in injuries severe enough to require medical attention. Your parents can decide what education you will receive, what your religion will be, what your name is, and where you live. Your father's home is your legal home unless the courts rule otherwise.

When you reach the age agreed upon in your province— it ranges from sixteen in Ontario to eighteen in Quebec— your parents can ask you to leave and they no longer are obliged to support you unless you are physically or emotionally disabled.

British Columbia's Berger Commission took a child's point of view on parental rights and concluded that parents often fail to meet the emotional, intellectual, and even physical needs of their children, sometimes deliberately but more often because they are uninformed about child development, have had deprived backgrounds themselves, are sunk in poverty, or can't find in the community the service the child needs.

The Commission therefore recommended that the government, which has the final responsibility in law for all children, should exercise it more vigorously. Parents who are unable or unwilling to provide

13   You are a child

health services, guidance, continuity and learnable education for their children should have government backup that will step in and remedy the situation on the child's behalf.

And children's rights, the Berger Commission added, should not be vulnerable to political caprice. Whenever a child is denied a basic right, the courts should have the power to order that the injustice be corrected by the appropriate municipal, provincial or federal body.

# 2 You are a wife

When two people marry they become one: him.

The trend in modern relationships is toward an egalitarian model of shared responsibility, but the matrimonial laws of the land are still rooted in centuries of master and captured maiden concepts. This fossil shapes the economics and the sexual choices affecting both parties immediately following the misty pronouncement that they are man and wife.

Man and *wife*. The inference is that the man is unchanged by the ceremony but the woman has become something other than she was. She is no longer herself, she is changed. The truth is that when the confetti and rice have been cleared away, it can be seen that in the legal sense both partners have been threatened with heavy consequences for certain misbehaviour and both have surrendered not only some of the freedom they had before the ceremony but much of their dignity as well.

Marriage certificates are legal documents. Despite the fact that they are almost always obtained without the advice of a lawyer and they cost only pennies, they are the most expensive, important, and diffi-cult-to-break contracts of a lifetime.

Marriage, in the legal sense only, is a purchase. The buyer is the man, who commits himself for the rest of his life to provide food, shelter, clothing, and medical attention in return for what he has ac-quired, which is explicitly the exclusive use of his bride's vagina. He is out of his part of the deal only if some other male uses his property.

The woman who remains celibate after a marriage break-up continues to deliver a crucial part of the bargain and therefore is enti-tled to continued support. As soon as another male gains access to her husband's property—which remains his even after the divorce— the contract is broken and the husband's financial obligation is over.

The marriage law, and such critical social agencies as welfare departments, take the view that the sexual apparatus of women is a money-maker. Whoever uses it pays.

From this degrading central concept come such laws as the one pertaining to rape: a wife cannot charge her husband with rape because that part of her is his property to claim as he pleases. He is not allowed to punch her in the eye: she can charge him with assault because her eye belongs to her. Her vagina, however, does not.

Also, if the wife has been injured in an accident and cannot fulfill her part of the agreement, which is to provide sexual access, the husband can sue the person responsible for this mishap to *him*. He is said in law to have lost consortium, which the law equates with a swindle. He's paying for something he's not getting.

If, however, the husband has been injured in an accident in such a way as to make sexual intercourse impossible for him, the wife may not sue. As far as Canadian law is concerned, her sex drive is non-existent.

In the United States, however, where Equal Rights Amendments to state constitutions have resulted in re-examination of many absurdities in Victorian laws, a wife in Pennsylvania in May 1974 obtained permission from the Supreme Court to sue for loss of consortium, a legal first.

Throughout a good deal of recorded history, society believed that a husband had title to his wife, exactly as he did to a slave he had purchased. If he wanted to, he could kill her. Until the middle of the nineteenth century, there was a category in law— bluntly defined as "women, children and lunatics"— which had no status. Marriage laws reflected this and the wedding ceremony was the straight transfer of child-bearing machinery from one owner, the father who guaranteed the intact hymen, to the new owner, the husband.

The marriage certificate remains philosophically unchanged, a statement of property rights. In recent years law reform commissions, women's organizations, and single-father groups have been recommending revisions in the matrimonial laws in order to reflect a less debased view of both men and women. Unfortunately, as with most legal change in Canada, the British North America Act with its gerrymandered division of federal and provincial jurisdictions complicates the problem. Marriage is whatever each province says it is.

There are sharp regional differences, with British Columbia usually far ahead of the country, Quebec improving creatively from some of the worst conditions, and the Maritimes snoozing in the salt mists. Some of the conditions relating to marriage, however, are almost identical everywhere. One of these concerns validity.

## Are you really married?

The most common reason for declaring a marriage to be invalid, by which a court declares that the marriage does not exist, is bigamy. It is bigamy and not marriage if one of the partners is legally married to someone else at the time of the second ceremony. Sometimes this can happen unintentionally, such as when the twice-married person believes that a divorce has taken place in another country.

A marriage is also invalid if it can be shown that one partner did not have the mental capacity to understand what the ceremony was all about, either by reason of insanity or mental retardation.

There are ancient taboos against interfamilial marriages which the law has codified. A marriage between certain relatives is a legal impossibility. The regulations vary slightly from one province to another but the list basically is this:

Marriage may not take place between father and daughter, son and mother, brother and sister, grandfather and granddaughter, grandson and grandmother, uncle and niece, nephew and aunt, daughter's husband and his mother-in-law, stepfather and stepdaughter, husband's father and his daughter-in-law, husband's son and his stepmother, husband's grandfather and his granddaughter-in-law, husband's grandson and his step-grandmother, husband's uncle and his niece-in-law, niece's husband and his aunt-in-law, granddaughter's husband and his grandmother-in-law, and grandmother's husband and his step-granddaughter.

Some of these forbidden marriages touch people who may have no blood relationship at all, while there are some curious omissions. Cousins, even first cousins, may legally marry, for instance. First cousins, however, are advised to consult a geneticist before starting a family. They may match up and reinforce some genetic defect.

In 1975 the Parliament of Canada approved the marriage of an uncle and his niece, over-ruling the law of their home province Quebec. Their blood relationship was tenuous: one of the half-brothers of the groom was the father of the bride.

Marriages can also be declared void if there is proof that the ceremony took place without the free will of both parties. Neither your parents nor anyone else can force you into a marriage. The condition of free will is crucial in the legality of marriage. However, it is rarely invoked in courts because evidence of coercion and threats is difficult to establish; it requires witnesses and perhaps medical testimony from a doctor who saw signs of physical abuse or from a psychiatrist with personal knowledge of the dark moods at the time.

The law regards all pressure to marry, even pressure that does not involve physical harm or the threat of it, as unlawful duress. Any threat which induces fear in you is duress and sufficient witnesses will enable you to subsequently have the ceremony nullified. It is easier in the long run to simply dig in your heels and refuse to marry, however.

A marriage isn't legal if it can be proved that one of the partners was under the influence of drugs or alcohol at the time of the ceremony to such a degree that there was no awareness of what was happening. There is also no marriage if someone unknowingly marries the wrong person, such as the twin of the intended mate or the substitution of someone else in an arranged marriage between strangers.

The principle of free will is strictly observed so far as legal marriage is concerned but the law doesn't consider it a violation of this principle if people misrepresent themselves to the partners they marry. For instance, the marriage is valid if the groom has been pretending to be wealthy during the courtship and turns out to be broke, or if he claims to be an occasional drinker and actually is a raving alcoholic. Misjudging the partner's character or financial status doesn't change the legality of the marriage and neither does the subsequent discovery that the bride was pregnant at the time— even if the groom is not the father of the child. It may be an unhappy relationship, but it is still a marriage.

There is a difference between what the law calls a void marriage and what is known as a voidable marriage. Void marriages are those which never had a legal existence: marriages against the free will of both parties are in this group. Either partner can apply to the courts for an annulment.

But a voidable marriage is one which was legal at the time of the ceremony but later is defaulted because there was no consummation. The Divorce Act of Canada states in Section Four that marriages which have not been consummated for the period of one year following the ceremony can be ended by divorce action; voiding the marriage is another process, one which falls in provincial jurisdiction, and it is peculiar in that it must be demonstrated that there was no sexual intercourse because it was impossible, either for physical or psychological reasons.

This excludes those odd cases in which the bride or groom have a change of heart immediately after the ceremony and separate before reaching the marriage bed. One young woman whose husband beat her bloody an hour after she married him discovered to her astonishment that she was legally married, even though he spent the wedding night in jail and she spent it in a hospital. She was obliged to proceed with a divorce, since her husband was capable of consummating the marriage.

To void a marriage it must be established that failure to consummate is due to impotence that cannot be cured by doctors or counsellors. There must be testimony from professionals, the nature of which is so humiliating to the male that most couples with genuine grounds for voiding their marriages prefer lengthier divorce procedures instead.

When an annulment is granted it acts retroactively to erase the marriage. Despite this, the non-husband may be required to maintain his non-wife by means of periodic payments or a lump sum. The Matrimonial Causes Act of Ontario has a section which enables a judge to require maintenance payments if the non-wife has not had intercourse with anyone since the non-wedding, thus fulfilling her part of the bargain.

A marriage may also be invalid if one of the parties is younger than the age of consent in the province in which the ceremony is performed and there has not been a consent form obtained from the appropriate parent. (See ARE YOU OLD ENOUGH?, page 21).

Despite all the above, Canadian courts have been known to forgive some breaches of the Marriage Act when it can be shown that the marriage took place in good faith. For instance, there was an Ontario case (Clause v. Clause) in which the bride was under eighteen years of age at the time of the ceremony and there was no record of a consent form. The bride's father couldn't recall whether or not he had signed one and the marriage was ruled valid.

In another case in Ontario the couple had overlooked the necessity to obtain a marriage license (Alspector v. Alspector). The marriage was ruled valid because it had been an honest mistake.

## Marriage license

Except in Newfoundland, where the Solemnization of Marriages Act makes no mention of pre-ceremony permits, you must have either a marriage license or the posting of banns before you can be married.

Marriage licenses are obtained at City Hall or some comparable municipal office, usually from the clerk. It will cost about $15 and must be dated a certain number of days before the ceremony is planned, a gap gracefully designed for cooling off impetuosity. Both parties must fill out the application forms in person; if this is impossible the one applying must have the absent one's birth certificate.

Most provinces also have a resident requirement. At least one of the partners must live in the province for an established period (in Ontario it is fifteen days, for example) before applying for a license.

Alberta also requires a medical certificate dated not earlier than two weeks prior to the application for a marriage license which states the negative result of blood tests for syphilis.

The reading and publishing of banns is equal to a marriage license in six provinces: Ontario, New Brunswick, Manitoba, Quebec, Saskatchewan, and British Columbia. The cleric announces the names of the couple and their intention to wed, at three successive Sabbath services and also issues this information in whatever printed form is customary in that denomination. The cleric then certifies that this has been properly done.

Nova Scotia and Alberta insist on a license, banns or not. Quebec recognizes either the clerical banns or a notice of intent to wed posted in the courthouse by a local clerk twenty days before the ceremony is to take place.

## The ceremony

The words spoken in the ceremony itself are not immutable, except in those faiths committed to orthodox tradition. Some aspects of the service, such as asking if anyone knows just cause why the marriage should not proceed, are obligatory and each faith requires certain phrases or paraphrases of dearly-treasured concepts, but beyond these fundamentals there is considerable latitude for creativity.

Couples can write their own services and stage them to suit themselves, so long as the cleric agrees.

In some cases the question, "Who gives this woman in marriage?" isn't asked. It suggests to some people that the bride is a hopeless ninny who would have had a difficult time finding the front of the church or temple if her father hadn't led her. In some ceremonies the question is asked and the bride responds herself. In others her parents both reply to it and then the question is asked of the groom and his parents respond.

The wedding of one couple was solemnized in a cathedral within a ring formed by all the family and wedding guests holding hands.

"I now pronounce you man and wife" is often changed to "husband and wife". Fewer women promise to obey: there are instead declarations of mutual respect, love, sharing, and individual growth. Some couples feel that "till death do us part" is an unrealistic vow, and either drop it entirely or substitute something along the lines of "as long as we both shall love".

One couple, married in a pioneer museum that had been a church a century ago, wrote a service which began, "The spiritual union of Margy and Garney has existed for many years. It is a reality. Through devoted love and intensive communication a strong sense of union has grown between them, and continues to grow. The legal union ... is not yet a reality. We are here to create this reality and share it."

The person who performs the ceremony can be a judge or magistrate in chambers if it is a civil service, or a member of the clergy of an established denomination if it is a religious service.

The service can be conducted anywhere that the officiating person agrees to, and at any time of the day or night, but civil ceremonies almost invariably are restricted to the judge's chambers and the normal nine to five workday.

But sky divers have been married in mid-air and circus performers on trapezes. Couples have been wed in meadows under the moon, on mountaintops, on beaches at sunrise, and in raucous pubs. Baroque or plain, it's all legal, and it's all full of hope.


## Are you old enough?

This is not an age deduced by behaviour psychologists or even by you in your infinite wisdom. Provincial and federal legislators have fixed the birthday upon which you are free to marry without consulting your parents or guardians. So far as the law is concerned, everyone past that date is mature enough to make such a momentous decision, and everyone short of it is incapable.

The definition of the age of consent to marriage not only varies from one province to another, but in some parts of the country your sex is a factor as well.

All those younger than the prescribed age of consent must obtain written permission before they can be married legally. There are a number of regulations to cover every imaginable contingency:

The father of the bride or groom is the one to give or withhold permission providing the parents are living together. The mother's opinion of the matter has no legal weight whatsoever.

The parent who has custody is the one to make the decision if the parents are divorced or separated.

Your surname determines the matter if your parents are living common-law. If it is your mother's surname, she decides; if you have been using your father or step-father's surname, he may exert the authority.

If you are a ward of the Crown or a child care agency, someone authorized by that guardian must sign the consent form.

The need for consent is waived if both parents are dead and there is no guardian, or if it can be demonstrated that the parent is irresponsible either by reason of mental illness or indifference to the child's well-being, or if the parent cannot be found after efforts have been made to do so.

If you are pregnant or if you have given birth to a baby, the judge probably will permit you to marry even if your parents disapprove. You are entitled to appeal to a judge if your parents or guardians refuse to give you permission to marry, but parenthood is almost the only situation which will almost invariably result in an overrule of their resistance. If you are able to prove that your parents have shown a consistent lack of consideration and concern for you, and have usually not acted in your best interests, the judge may grant you consent to marry over their objections.

The common law forbids the marriage of girls younger than twelve or boys younger than fourteen. Provincial rulings do not fall below this alarming baseline but exceptions have been made when there is a pregnancy.

Pregnancy has become an escape route for some adolescents who are acutely unhappy at home or at school. By becoming pregnant they can gain automatic adult status: babies become a ticket to travel.

All adolescents are a volatile mixture of idealism, optimism, impulsiveness, terror and loneliness. It is natural to their stage of development to have romantic visions of eternal love. Their easy access to a marriage contract therefore betrays many of them into ill-considered weddings. There were 56,586 teen-aged girls married in Canada in 1973; in the same year there were 13,081 weddings involving both a teen-aged bride and a teen-aged groom. Marriages between young people have the highest casualty rate in the country.

## What's your name?

The law does not oblige you to take your husband's name when you marry. It is the custom, known for a century as "the unity of legal personality" but it is not obligatory. The law is so unclear on this matter that women who haven't used their maiden names for thirty years have been able to resurrect it simply by declaring that they want to. The old English common law upheld the right of citizens to give themselves whatever name they liked, so long as it was not done to defraud anyone, and women in recent years have been doing just that.

It is use which gives your name validity. If you are about to be married and wish to continue your birth name, you can do so without effort. With a few exceptions your husband's name does not need to play any part in your legal identity.

If you have been using your husband's name for any length of time, the situation is somewhat different. His name is legally yours: your credit rating will be filed in his folder and you'll have to start from scratch to establish credit in the new name. In order to change your name on existing deeds, wills, insurance policies and the like, you'll have to apply for a legal change of name. The hitch is that most provinces require family unanimity so far as names are concerned: if you change your name to your birth name, your husband and children must take the same name.

The law allows you to resume your birth name when you are divorced. This is automatic and you don't have to apply for an official change of name. You may not revert to your birth name if you are separated, however, so long as your husband is contributing to your support—unless he agrees to it.

When you marry, if you plan to use your husband's name, your passport in your birth name is no longer valid and you must apply for a new one which gives your husband's name. His old passport, however, continues in force.

Complain to your Member of Parliament. Explain that marriage does not make you less of a citizen.

Credit bureaus are resistant to women reclaiming their birth names. Some may justify their opposition by telling you that your husband is responsible for your debts and therefore must stand behind your credit. This is nonsense. Your husband is responsible only for those debts that you incur in order to provide yourself with the essentials of survival, such as food, shelter and clothing, and only in certain circumstances to do with your sexual fidelity.

If you have a problem with credit card issuers—and you will —obtain copies of your birth certificate and mail these with your application for a new card. It is irrefutable proof of your identity.

This informal way of repatriating your name is the simpler method. The 1975 President of the National Action Committee of the Status of Women, Lorna Marsden, reached back four generations and picked her maternal grandmother's maiden name for her own after twenty-odd years of having her father's name and a number of years after that of using her husband's name. When she discovered that the legal change of name procedure was unworkable, she changed her name by fiat: announced it to her friends and associates, changed those documents that could be changed, and found that acceptance was almost painless.

The Ontario Women's Bureau of the Ministry of Labour circulated a sample letter that one woman sent to creditors and government agencies. It read:

"Please let it be known to all persons, that after eleven years of frustration and being identified under a foreign alias to which I could never learn to relate, I am finally free of my DP handle and as of right now, Ms. Sandy Zwegers is no longer Ms. Sandy Zwegers, but is ... MS. SANDY PROWSE!!!!

"I have reverted back to my very own name that I was born with and am thrilled to ask you to please change your records accordingly. My husband is backing up this decision and believes in my crusade 100%. The next body to refer to me as Mrs. Albert Zwegers *will be sorry.*"

Another woman whose Eaton's credit card was labelled Mrs. Ed Fitzgerald wrote the company sweetly to explain that her name wasn't Ed. "My husband and I have an agreement," she said. "I don't use his name and he doesn't use mine."

Some couples are using composite names. The most common technique is the hyphenated name, as in Webster-Zaretski. It is cumbersome, however, and presents some problems to the next generation, particularly if a child with a double birth name happens to marry someone similarly endowed.

It's interesting that Icelandic people have individual surnames and keep them. A woman doesn't change her name upon marriage and the children are given surnames of their own.

Another option that some couples in Canada have adopted is to blend their surnames to create an exotic name such as Webski or Zarster. One couple invented the notion of using his last name for both of them half of the year and her last name for them both the rest of the time. This turned out to be a wholly untenable arrangement.

One woman who had been married three times and divorced three times gave some exhausted thought to the four changes of name, all of them a man's name, that she had experienced in her lifetime. She therefore decided on a new name. She is now, and forever, simply Heather Elizabeth.

Your children's legal surname is their father's unless you are single. Children of unmarried women normally use their mother's birth name. If you later want to change the children's birth names from that of their father, you must have his permission to do so. If the children are older than twelve, they must be consulted also.

Consult a lawyer when considering a legal change of name. This area of the law is a labyrinth of implications.

## Is marriage a good idea?

It is and it isn't. The woman who lives with her love without a marriage ceremony has more autonomy in law but less economic protection for herself and her children. It makes perfect sense from the point of view of human dignity that grown women should not be dependent on the earnings of men, but in fact women's wages and promotion opportunities are still so inferior to those of men that self-sufficiency usually results in a lower standard of living for women, which makes marriage economically a superior arrangement.

Example: The National Council of Welfare reported on children in poverty in Canada in March 1975. The report, *poor kids*, revealed that in one-parent families headed by men, thirty-four per cent of the children lived below the poverty line; in one-parent families headed by women, sixty-nine per cent lived in poverty.

From a legal standpoint, marriage restricts the freedom of both men and women. Both give up a range of choices when they marry. The woman is tied to the income level of her mate, she must live where he lives, she must be sexually monogamous. The man is tied financially to someone who may or may not give value for what she receives.

On the other hand there are certain advantages to marriage. The man who lives in a common-law arrangement cannot claim his partner as a dependent for an income tax exemption, while a married man can. A woman living common-law must pay her own provincial health insurance; she and her mate cannot obtain the cheaper family coverage.

Tax experts, however, note that when both partners are working there is an advantage to the common-law state, especially if there are children. Inventing a couple, Bob with an income of $20,000 and Sally with an income of $8,000, both raising two children of their own from previous marriages, one tax specialist discovered that Bob could claim a $3,286 tax exemption if the couple was married in 1975 and Sally one for $1,878. If they lived common-law, however, each claiming one child as a dependent, Bob would have a tax exemption of $3,874 and Sally an exemption of $2,582, for a saving of $517.

In addition Bob can hire Sally and deduct her wages as an expense for tax purposes if they are not married. If they are married, the tax department expects Sally to contribute her labour free.

It isn't difficult to evaluate marriage in pragmatic financial terms but the institution, as everyone knows, transcends ledger books. There is societal reinforcement and respect for the married couple but only doubtful acceptance and much uneasiness about couples living together without marriage. The feeling that marriage is a sacred and social union is deeply rooted. Many believe the ceremony represents not only a higher level of integrity and commitment but also certain spiritual and ethic values. In such a rich tapestry it is unrealistic to examine only the financial benefits or the legal obligations, like carping about the quality of the paper on which heavenly poetry is written. This, however, is a book about the law.

These are the legal benefits of living common-law:

You exist. Your passport remains valid. You will not have arguments with credit bureaus and government agencies over the question of your reality.

The children you bear will have your name and you will have sole authority in such areas as medical treatment, school leaving, where they will live, or whether or not they can marry while under the age of consent.

If your mate moves to another place, you are not obligated to follow in order to protect your right to be supported. Since you have no such right you will not be tempted to tag along against your better judgment. Also, you can have another sexual partner without running the risk of a full discussion of your morals by two lawyers and a judge.

You are not entirely without rights. In November 1974, an Ontario court ruled that a woman who had lived for twenty-eight years in a common-law relationship was entitled to an estate of close to $60,000, rather than the $500 that her common-law partner had stipulated in his will.

British Columbia has recognized common-law relationships of more than two years' duration. According to the Family Relations Act of 1972, one spouse in such a relationship cannot refuse or neglect "without reasonable excuse" to provide reasonable support and maintenance for the other spouse when they part.

These are the legal benefits of marriage:

Unlike the woman who isn't married you are probably entitled to some protection if your marriage fails. Providing you are sexually faithful and do not desert, your marriage certificate may assure you of lifelong support payments.

You are entitled to food, shelter, clothing, and medical and legal services. If your husband doesn't provide these staples, you are entitled to buy them anyway and charge them to his account. At present he is not entitled to do the same if you are the wage earner and he is broke.

In the event of his death you are likely to inherit.

Your children are described in law as legitimate, which gives them automatic rights to inherit. If you are not employed, your husband is obligated to provide the necessities of life for the children.

## Can he beat you?

With moderation. The police and judges have their own slide-rules to determine the definition of a moderate beating. Divorces for cruelty are not granted on the basis of a single beating or even scattered beatings. One judge in Scotland in January 1975 admonished a husband for punching his wife on the jaw. He commented, "It is a well-known fact that you can strike your wife's bottom if you wish, but you must not strike her on the face."

He added kindly, "I believe that reasonable chastisement should be the duty of every husband if his wife misbehaves."

We have not come very far from the law two centuries old which permitted husbands to beat their wives so long as it was not done in a "violent or cruel manner", an era in which it was not considered discourteous for a husband to keep his wife in chains.

Modern laws adhere to the principle that adults should not harm one another physically unless they are married. A woman, for instance, cannot charge her husband with rape.

If your husband strikes you, you may call a policeman and lay a charge of assault against him. Policemen are reluctant to proceed with such domestic disputes because of the high number of cases subsequently dropped. It is possible to ask for the protection of the law if your husband threatens to hit you.

The obvious hazard here is that an abusive husband is unlikely to be pleased that his wife has called the police. Unless you have somewhere else to live, you may be in danger of more beatings. Should you persevere with the charge, laws that prohibit a wife testifying against her husband are waived. If he is convicted the judge often does not impose any sentence: he warns the man to stop it or he'll be fined or jailed the next time. Did you know that most of the murderers in Canada are men and most of their victims are their wives or girl friends?

# Where do you live?

You live wherever your husband decides. If his job takes him to another community, you and the children must accompany him or else you are said to have deserted, in which case you may lose your right to financial support and your share of his property. If your job requires a move, he doesn't have to follow. If you go anyway, it's desertion.

You can appeal to the court if your husband is demanding that you move to a climate that will be injurious to your health, or to a place where you cannot obtain the specialized medical treatment you need. If the court rules in your favour, your husband will have to continue to support you in your present location and you have not deserted him.

You can also ask the court to help you if you are being asked to live with someone you detest; for instance, if your husband wants you to share your home with an odious relative.

# Can you sue him?

Most provinces are moving, or have moved, to change the law which prevents you from suing your husband if his carelessness has resulted in a serious injury to you. This means a new attitude is evolving within insurance companies, which in the past did not have to pay liability on "third party" policies whenever two of the three parties were husband and wife—the law maintained that the husband and wife were not two people, they were one.

It was possible to claim damages against your husband if he kicked your dog and crippled it but not if he did the same thing to you.

This same concept that a husband and wife are one person— him—results in such laws as the one which does not allow you to be charged as an accessory after the fact to any crime your husband commits or to be arrested for helping him escape; you are, you see, *part* of him.

Similarly you can't sue him for slander or libel and nothing you say to him can result in a suit for slander or libel, since communication between husband and wife is privileged.

If you loan money to your husband or enter into any contract with him to his benefit, you can move to have it nullified because the law takes the sympathetic view that you might have signed under duress or ignorance. This is the reason banks require women co-signing loans for their spouses to obtain the advice of a lawyer. The bank manager will explain that this is necessary "to make sure you understand the legal consequences", but actually it provides the bank with the evidence it needs to hold you to the agreement. If you don't see a lawyer, it can't.

If you are injured in an accident you can sue the person responsible—and so can your husband if the injuries disable you and your husband loses your "services".

If you and your husband both own cars and they collide, he cannot sue you for negligence. Curiously, you can sue him.

These inequities in the law are among the easiest injustices for legislators to correct and are being revised in most provinces. The law about colliding spouses, for instance, has been revised in Ontario.

## What do you own?

You are entitled to keep whatever property you had before your marriage, whatever you have inherited during the marriage and whatever gifts were given to you, providing you can establish that they were intended for you alone and not to be shared. If you have earned money of your own and banked it in an account in your own name, you can keep this. If you have been spending your own money on car payments or whatever, you will need receipts to establish your equity.

If you brought nothing into the marriage, if you have been a home-bound housewife and mother ever since the ceremony, it is entirely possible that you will be found by the courts to own nothing and be entitled to nothing.

The patron saint of whatever changes have occurred or may occur in your province concerning matrimonial property is a shy Alberta ranchwoman, Irene Murdoch. In the 1940s she used money of her own to help her husband purchase farm property. After that he was absent five months of the year at other employment while she took care of the chores alone, "haying, raking, swathing, mowing, driving trucks and tractors and teams, quietening horses, taking cattle back and forth to the reserve, dehorning, vaccinating, branding, anything that was to be done . . ." She was beaten by her husband so severely that she had to be hospitalized and there is permanent damage to her face and speech.

When the Murdochs separated, the courts of the land right up to the Supreme Court of Canada unconscionably stripped Irene Murdoch of any claim to the ranch. They ruled that her husband owns it all and she is now a welfare recipient. The Supreme Court judges, with Chief Justice Bora Laskin dissenting, decided that her husband was entitled to her free labour all those years and no recompense was justified.

The shock of that decision is still being felt. There has been a quickened interest in reform ever since the Murdoch v. Murdoch case.

Matrimonial property is that property which is purchased during the marriage by either husband alone, wife alone or husband and wife together. In the past, when very few wives worked outside their homes after marriage, all the property technically belonged to husbands. The wage-earner had title to everything, the one giving free labour had nothing.

Quebec led Canada in reforming the matrimonial property laws in 1970. A regime of "Partnership of Acquests" was established on the day the legislation was enacted and since then all property purchased by married people, jointly or singly, belongs to them both if the marriage breaks up. The hitch is that during the marriage the purchaser of the property has full control of it. If a divorce appears imminent, a wife cannot prevent her husband from disposing of property that will be one-half hers in any divorce settlement. This, however, applies only to movable property, such as a car; a husband cannot sell a house or a business without his wife's consent.

The legislation applies only to marriages that took place after July 1, 1970.

When divorce courts divide property in those provinces without matrimonial property reform, they can only examine who paid for what and rule accordingly. The non-wage-earning housewife is dispossessed and very often so is the wage-earning wife. Many families fall into the pattern of his money going to pay for mortgage installments and the stereo, while hers is used for consumables such as groceries and vacations. He ends up with all the property receipts, which gives him sole ownership.

Accordingly British Columbia and the Northwest Territories were the first to give divorce courts discretionary power to carve the property as seems fair, rather than on the basis of one spouse's claim. England and New Zealand have similar legislation. The English law, for instance, has regard for the contributions made by each party to the marriage's well-being, "including any contribution made by looking after the home or caring for the family."

New Zealand, further, has "no fault" divorce which does not permit one spouse to be paupered because of misconduct. The heart of Canadian divorce law is punitive: courts attempt to discover which partner is to blame, which is the evil one, and on this basis decide on maintenance and the custody of children. In practice women who leave their husbands or have sexual relations outside of marriage are heavily penalized, while no comparable punishment falls on men who leave their wives or have sexual relations outside of marriage.

A favoured divorce reform has been described as *deferred sharing*, by which partners have title to whatever they purchase during the marriage but must share title when they obtain a divorce. Upon the dissolution of the marriage all assets are totalled, the current debts are subtracted, along with the *value* of property owned before the marriage or gifted specifically to one partner, and the rest is split in two equal parts. This division includes the increased value of any property owned before the marriage.

Deferred sharing regimes exist in Denmark, Sweden, Norway, Finland, West Germany and Holland and Quebec, while many other provinces have similar recommendations before the legislatures.

If your province does not yet have matrimonial property reform you are entitled only to what is called dower rights. So long as you haven't deserted the home and have been chaste, you can claim one-third of your husband's real property. You lose this right if you have a lover and dower rights do not have to be part of a divorce settlement.

They are active mainly during the marriage. Your husband may not sell the house or the farm without your consent unless he pays you one-third of the proceeds. You cannot stop him from selling the property so long as he gives you this share. In one unhappy case, the one-third was not paid to the wife but was given to the Court for disposal.

If your husband deserts, you can remain in the family home even if it is in his name, at least until he provides suitable alternative accommodation. If you desert or commit adultery, you may forfeit your dower rights and any claim for financial support except for your children.

So long as you are faithful and living with your husband, you can pledge his credit. You are permitted to buy necessities of life without his approval and he must pay for them.

But the court must be satisfied that you buy only "things that are really necessary and suitable to the style in which the husband chooses to live, in so far as the articles fall fairly within the domestic department which is ordinarily confined to the management of the wife." Kitchen equipment is your bailiwick, the living room and den are probably his.

The tricky part is the phrase, "the style in which the husband chooses to live". If your husband lives beyond his means, for instance, you are permitted purchases in the same price range. If your husband is wealthy but lives shabbily, you cannot buy anything expensive.

No matter how unreasonable, your husband's chosen lifestyle

is your compulsory lifestyle. Providing you observe this requirement, you can buy food and clothing for yourself and the children, household equipment for cleaning, laundry and cooking, medical and legal services and medicine.

Unless you earn money of your own, everything you buy is legally his. Even the money you save out of your housekeeping allowance is his by law, including the interest on it. If you save enough to purchase property and purchase it in your own name, he can claim it; it is his.

## How much are you worth?

Not much. (See above.) There are proposals that women who work at home as housekeepers and tenders of children should be paid a fair salary, should receive vacations with pay, should be covered by workmen's compensation laws and the Canada Pension Plan, and when they are ill they should be entitled to sickness benefits just like everyone else in the work force.

The first argument against paying housewives is the cost. Statistics Canada said that there were 3.9 million women keeping house in Canada in 1972. Some sort of minimum guaranteed income plan would cost the government $19 billion to give each housewife $5,000 a year.

The other argument is the one that prizes voluntary labour as the voice of altruism and conscience. It is observably true that the work ethic hasn't changed much in Canada in recent years but the work-for-pay ethic has. An increasing number of people of all ages, but especially those in their twenties, are working their heads off stripping floors, planting gardens, staffing distress centres—all without pay. Significantly, when the Metropolitan Toronto Zoo laid off a number of employees in a budget cutback in 1975, they all turned up for work the next day anyway.

However, it is equally true that there is something symbolic about having money of your own. Women who volunteer to head big-budget social agency boards or run complex fund-raising drives somehow never think of themselves as skilled and competent in the same way that working-for-wages women do. The free labour of women, particularly in the child-raising area of their activities, is generally downgraded by everyone, including the women themselves, and spills over to keep salaries in day-care centres unrealistically low. If housewives were paid for raising children, offered child-raising courses to upgrade their skills and relief staff to permit them some leisure, there is no question but that the lives of mothers and children would be improved.

In the meantime, the Status of Women Commission has observed that "more goods and services are produced without pay in the home than anywhere else." The United States has estimated that the free labour of housewives is equivalent to twenty-four per cent of the Gross National Product. More than one economist has noted that the failure to include the free labour of women in the GNP gives a false picture of a country's productivity.

One recent estimate of the value of an individual housewife's contribution set the figure at $257.53 a week, or $13,391.56 a year, if husbands had to purchase professional cleaners, laundry services, cooks and child-care workers, not to mention the exclusively available non-refusable sex.

Many wives help in their husband's occupations as well as performing household tasks. City wives weigh apples and keep the books, country wives feed the stock, coastal wives clean fish. For the most part there is no pay; wives who work for their husbands are not entitled to the same benefits as other working women. To get around this, the men of one Maritime fishing village are hiring one another's wives as helpers.

Sylva Gelber, director of the Women's Bureau of the federal Department of Labour, has been campaigning for inclusion of the housewife's contribution to the national economy in the GNP. She believes that this will focus attention on the enormous contribution of women.

"They represent a substantial percentage of the national income," Gelber says. "The belittling of the role of the housewife and of household domestic service has been responsible in no small part for many of the dissatisfactions being experienced by some younger women who might well have found satisfaction in choosing such a role, but for prevailing attitudes."

*The Last Post* commented, "The fact that housework, the occupation of the majority of women and the prototype of all women's work, is unpaid, is the source of the financial dependency of women upon men, of the societal structure of domination which is reproduced within the supposedly private confines of the home. Wages for housework is not just a demand for justice in an unjust society; the wages for all houseworkers is a pre-condition for a feminist movement."

Occasionally there is a case before the court which requires a judge to place a price on the services of a wife, such as in suits for damages for what the law quaintly calls "criminal conversion", meaning that foul play has robbed the husband of said services.

33   You are a wife

Some years ago a judge in Pennsylvania was ruling on the case of a man whose deceased wife had helped in his restaurant in the capacity of cook and attendant, as well as functioning as housekeeper and mate. The judge was deeply moved.

"The loss of a wife's services," he said, "are imponderables which, indeed, command almost inestimable values. The companionship which a wife brings to a husband in the daily routine and conduct of living, her encouraging glance or invigorating smile at times of anxiety or weakness—when the dull thud and clash of industrial and economic competition have brought nerve and sinew to a breaking point. . . ." Wonderful.

Most judges merely calculate the replacement value of the wife's services at the going rate, subtract the cost of her maintenance, and skip the poetry. Whatever the amount, it is more than she ever saw while she was on her feet.

Mr. Justice Edson Haines of the Supreme Court of Ontario made a significant ruling in the spring of 1975 when he was presented with the case of a suit for damages by a man and his children after the wife and mother had been killed in an automobile accident.

The woman was described as a housewife who had never made a financial contribution to the household, which usually is significant to the case of the defense. For instance, the Supreme Court of Canada in 1967 awarded a nine-year-old $2,000 and a twelve-year-old $1,000 for the loss of their mother, an amount which represented an *increase* over the award of a lower court.

Mr. Justice Haines, however, observed that the woman in the case before him "encouraged and sustained her husband in his work" and that she was "the cornerstone, providing incentive, encouragement, counsel and advice" for her entire family. He made an award of the highest amount ever allowed in Canada for the loss of a housewife-mother, $50,000.

## Can you write your own contract?

Yes. Right now, if you want to, whether you are about to be married or have been in a marriage for thirty years. You don't have to wait for the province of your choice to pass more equitable matrimonial property laws: you can do it yourself, with a fair likelihood that the contract will be respected.

You should have an independent lawyer, one who has had no prior dealings with either one of you and one not bound by friendship to either. This will avoid any later charge of bias. You must both feel comfortable about all the provisions. If the marriage breaks down and one of you claims to have been forced into the agreement, or wheedled or nagged into signing, the judge will be upset.

The contract can cover assets owned by each before the marriage and assets acquired after, or anticipated. You can agree to merge ownership of everything equally, or you can stipulate and describe exactly what belongs to him and what belongs to you.

You can waive your right to financial dependency if autonomy is your preference. The two of you can agree to keep your incomes separate but divide the expenses in half, or you may decide to put your money in a joint bank account and pay the bills from it, or you may wish to pay expenses on a scale proportionate to your incomes if one of you has a much larger salary than the other.

You can set out your preference concerning alimony and maintenance. If you don't believe it is fair for either of you to be financially encumbered by the other if the marriage should fail, you can declare this. You can also state that all children of your dissolved union will be supported by both of you, on a scale proportionate to your incomes.

These provisions will be considered by the judge who hears your divorce action but they are not binding on the decision. If you later feel differently about your concessions in the contract, the judge may rule in your favour that it is not in your best interest or that of your children to respect its provisions.

The contract can cover matters which do not involve money or property. You can put down how you feel about having children. If you want to wait a few years, or agree that neither of you wants to have children at all, you can establish which one will be responsible for birth control or else decide that the responsibility will be mutual.

The contract can also state areas of independence that are important to you, such as whether sexual fidelity is expected, whether invitations to one of you will automatically mean that both attend, whether you will spend a certain amount of time apart, and how two careers will either be dovetailed or given an order of precedence.

There could also be a category by a title such as "Care and Use of Living Space" which would outline how household tasks will be shared, with a daily or weekly schedule outlining the division of labour.

Contracts can have expiry dates, or can have a clause outlining the circumstances under which they will be renegotiated, or giving the appeals procedure, or naming an arbitrator. One couple decided in advance that they would have three children, live together for twenty years in order to raise them, and then part so each could pick up independent development. They did exactly that, right on schedule.

One young woman about to marry a man who had a tendency to drink too much put this clause in the contract: that she would warn him only once at a party that he was becoming drunk and should switch to ginger ale; that if he continued to drink alcohol she would leave the party alone and he would not be permitted to come home for three days, upon which she was not to refer to the incident at all.

A sample contract circulated widely in British Columbia avoids the word marriage. Instead the parties enter into what they term a "meaningful relationship," the contract for which includes a clause covering the surname or surnames the couple will use, another which states that children born on even days are the responsibility of one party and children born on odd days are the responsibility of the other, and a clause which states that meaningful communication shall be attempted at all times—except when one of the parties doesn't feel like it.

## Can you change your mind before the wedding?

Society is less concerned today than it used to be with bruises to reputation or ego that may result from being jilted. Suits for damages in such cases are rarely filed, but it is still a fact in law that engagements are contracts. Consequently, breaking an engagement is a breach of contract.

Lawyers for the defense will claim that there was pressure on the jilter to enter into the engagement, that it wasn't done freely, or else that there was misrepresentation or mental instability or the party was under age. It used to horrify judges if it was established that the woman was not a virgin, and therefore a poor marital risk. Some men still feel strongly that this deflowering is sufficient grounds to break off an engagement but courts no longer are sympathetic unless there is some other situation of more significance established.

Many countries have abolished the right to sue for breach of promise to marry, and such reform is expected soon in Canada. With or without it, there are certain customs generally observed when engagements are broken. If you are the one who calls it off, you should return the ring. If he breaks the engagement you can keep the ring if you want to, especially if you have gone to some expense so far as wedding invitations and a wedding dress and he refuses to compensate you. All wedding and shower gifts should be returned to the senders promptly.

# Second marriages

Dr. Johnson commented that "to marry a second time represents a triumph of hope over experience," but second marriages tend to have a better success rate than first ones when money problems are absent. Second marriages, however, are somewhat more complicated legally.

If you were divorced by a Special Act of the Parliament of Canada, you must file a copy of the Act certified by the proper officer with the Issuer of Marriage Licenses at City Hall.

If your divorce was granted by a court, or your marriage annulled by a court, you must have the Final Decree or Judgment of the Court with you when you apply for the marriage license, or else a copy of the document certified by the proper Court Officer. It isn't sufficient to have a copy of the Decree Nisi.

If your divorce or annulment took place outside Canada, you will need the authorization of the Provincial Secretary or that functionary's equivalent. Provincial regulations vary and none are simple. Consult a lawyer.

# 3 You are a mother

You must register your baby's name. The Vital Statistics Act indicates that a child "shall" be registered within thirty days of birth but a delay up to a year is permissible. The Family Allowance payments don't begin until the baby is registered, however. They will be retroactive to the date of birth.

The baby is registered on a form that shows your name only. It does not indicate whether or not you are married. If you are married you are not allowed to use your birth name on your child's registration: the surname must be your husband's. If you are not married, the baby's surname is the same as yours. The baby's father can register the birth in his name if you agree, but if that happens the registration will give your status as single. If you marry the baby's father subsequently you can obtain a new registration which will remove the entry of "single".

The law puts the responsibility for the baby's food, clothing and shelter on the father, unless the mother is employed and can share the expense. This applies whether or not you are married to him, providing in the case of unmarried parents that he admits paternity. He is obliged to provide for the child until the child is sixteen and this obligation remains even if you marry someone else.

Section 197 of the Criminal Code specifies that every parent, foster parent, guardian or head of the family must provide the necessaries of life for a child under the age of sixteen. The head of the family is often a woman living without a spouse. Canada has 378,000 women who are heads of single-parent families. Most of them, sixty-nine per cent, live below the poverty line. It is almost impossible to enforce court orders to extract maintenance allowances from fathers to help these women raise their children.

There are penalties for fathers who refuse to pay either fines or prison sentences. In practice, however, the fathers are either elusive or broke, usually both.

# The battered baby

Section 43 of the Criminal Code of Canada states: "Every school teacher, parent, or person standing in the place of a parent is justified in using force by way of correction towards a pupil or child, as the case may be, who is under his care, if the force does not exceed what is reasonable under the circumstances."

It is the legal sanction for what is central to child-raising techniques in most Canadian homes, the concept that children will behave better if they are hurt. There is considerable evidence that the opposite is true, but inflicting pain continues to be a major disciplinary method. When it is used to excess, as happens generally in situations where the adult is under severe stress, it is called child abuse.

Since World War II, Canadian provinces have been enacting and amending what is known as battered baby legislation, encouraging doctors, neighbours, teachers, and even bystanders, to report cases of suspected child abuse. There was considerable resistance to the new laws in the beginning from people who complained that they invaded the privacy of the family, invited meddlers and cranks, and interfered with a parent's right to discipline a child.

No one questions the child abuse laws any more except the growing number of people who want to strengthen them. Mary Van Stolk, author of *The Battered Child in Canada*, is an indefatigable leader of the movement to make it compulsory for people to report all cases of suspected child abuse or else be punished. She maintains, and no one disputes her, that only a fraction of all child-battering cases comes to the attention of authorities because of Canadian reluctance to get involved.

Quebec has new legislation which does impose penalties on people who fail to report child abuse they clearly knew about. Such legislation does work: in New York City when it was imposed, the number of reported cases of child battering tripled in two years. The element of punishment makes nurses, doctors, school teachers, and neighbours less likely to give parents the benefit of the doubt when they see a child with broken bones and bruises, and are informed that she "fell downstairs".

The arguments against such a law begin with enforcement: it is difficult to prove that someone should have reported child battering if the person insists that there seemed to be a logical reason for the injuries. There are also concerns that central registries of all child injuries will catch in its electronic net children of devoted parents whose broken bones or contusions really *did* happen in a fall down the stairs. Once on such a registry, it may be impossible for such an error to be corrected.

There is also the obvious failure of society to evolve any wonderful or even competent response to the problem of child battering. The old technique used to consist invariably of removing the child from a threatening home, but it was observed as years went by that displaced children frequently fail to thrive. In recent years the trend has been to leave children in their homes but maintain a child care agency watchdog and counselling service. This is slow, one-to-one, disheartening work but sometimes works a small miracle; other times it fails dramatically and the child is beaten to death.

Child care agencies have a mandate to remove the child from a life-threatening situation, either on a permanent or temporary custody basis, whichever the court decides. They may also use the alternatives of counselling, day care, regular visits, homemaker services, or whatever else seems likely to relieve the tension in the home and help the child. This, naturally, is extremely expensive.

Child abusers usually are immature, distraught people who were abused themselves as children. They have low flash points and aching needs for love and support, which an ungrateful, crying baby disappoints. Only a fraction of them are horrors, sadists who deliberately torture children for their own enjoyment. Most of the people who lose control and throw children against a wall do so under intolerable stress conditions, provoked often because the child wouldn't stop crying, or dirtied a diaper, or spilled a drink. Alcohol and poverty often figure in child abuse cases.

Child abuse cases are heartaches for everyone concerned, and a legal mess for judges. No lawyer represents the child, which leaves the possibility that child care agencies with tight budgets may not be pressing to provide the costly intervention the child needs. The parents often claim that the injury was the result of an accident, or that the circumstances which led to the child abuse will never happen again— either of which may be true.

To make matters more difficult, Family Court records and transcripts are not available for judges or lawyers to study in order to examine precedents. All decisions occur in a vacuum.

The House of Commons decided in December 1974 that the Standing Committee on Health, Welfare and Social Affairs should look into the state of the abused child in Canada. It was agreed that child abuse extended beyond a physical blow to the child and included that larger number of children who are emotionally deprived by parents who reject or neglect them, and those whose health and intelligence is permanently impaired because of malnutrition diets deficient in calorie-protein, a not-uncommon disaster in low income families.

Both emotional deprivation and early malnutrition have life-long consequences. Adults who suffered from either hardship as very young children are forever vulnerable in health and spirit. They are as severely damaged—perhaps more so—than those who were savagely beaten.

The National Law Reform Commission has examined new laws which would give children a guarantee of a minimum standard of care that would preserve their health and sanity. It is a tricky area, since it presumes to invade the rights of parents. Meanwhile, only one form of destruction of children is expressly forbidden, and that is the area known as battering.

There are a number of self-help groups in Canada which offer comfort and support to parents who have beaten their children or are fearful that they may. They have such names as Parents Anonymous or Parent-Child Concern. Some consist entirely of parents who describe themselves as child-abusers, others include some professional input.

Some parents are high risk. If you were beaten as a child, if you are a teen-ager without family resources, if you are poor, if your children are too closely spaced, if you live above the sixth floor in a high rise or in any congested space, if your baby was premature, you may be in trouble. Contact your local public health nurse, or a community information centre, or a distress centre, or the social worker at a children's hospital. You can call a child care agency without fear that it will result in your baby being taken away. They went out of the baby-snatching business years ago.

## You aren't married

The church felt so strongly about babies born out of wedlock in medieval England that their existence was almost obliterated. The child had no right to support from either parent and could not inherit. The term for such children was *filius nullius* and it turned out to be as drastic as it sounds. Most babies died of neglect.

We live in the shadow of that moral condemnation. Children born to unmarried mothers have legal and economic disadvantages. They may not inherit from their fathers unless they are named in the will. In some provinces they may not inherit from their mothers either if there are living "legitimate" children. Until recently the death of an illegitimate child was not considered a loss; if it happened through negligence, the mother could not sue.

If the father admits paternity, and therefore is described in law as the putative father, he must support the child until the age of sixteen, as well as paying medical expenses incurred during the pregnancy and childbirth. You can take legal action against him if he fails to provide for the child he has acknowledged; your chances of collecting are poor.

Your testimony alone will not be considered sufficient evidence of his paternity if he denies it. There must be other material evidence, of which the best known are the blood tests which have figured prominently in the paternity suits involving Hollywood stars. However, these tests are not conclusive evidence except when they prove that the man could *not* be the father.

If the family court grants an affiliation order asserting that the man is indeed the putative father, the next step will be to assess his income and determine how much he can afford for his child's support. The amount is adjusted to take into account your willingness or ability to help provide for the child.

If the putative father dies before the child is sixteen, his estate may continue to honour the terms of the affiliation order. It is always administered by a child care agency designated by the court. Money paid as the result of an affiliation agreement does not go directly into the mother's bank account.

In general, the law is not sympathetic to unmarried mothers. A provincial Court of Appeal only recently ruled that the mother of an "illegitimate" boy could not claim damages for his death by negligence. The Supreme Court of Canada declared in 1931 and again in 1967 that "the natural parent has no right to claim damages arising from the death of an illegitimate child." The Fatal Accidents Act of Alberta has been amended to remove this barbarity, and other provinces are following suit.

You have first claim on your child, but an increasing number of putative fathers are filing custody claims against unmarried mothers. To succeed, they must prove that the mother is unfit. If the mother has left the baby with the father for any length of time, or with anyone else, it may be seen by a court as evidence of her disinterest.

The Supreme Court of Canada in June 1975 upheld the right of a putative father who appealed a child care agency order in Edmonton that would have placed his two "illegitimate" children in a foster home. The case worker informed him that he wasn't a parent and could not interfere; the court ruled otherwise.

# Your baby is placed for adoption

If you decide during the pregnancy that you would like to place your baby for adoption, contact a Children's Aid Society right away. Your religion will influence your choice: Roman Catholic agencies take care of the babies of Roman Catholic mothers and some cities have Jewish agencies which provide for Jewish mothers. All other faiths, and those with no religious affiliation, go to the regular CAS. The religion of the father does not take precedent over yours.

The adoption must have the written consent "of every person who is a parent or guardian or who has custody or control or who is liable to contribution or support." These papers may be signed after the baby is seven days old. You are allowed a further period of three weeks or more to change your mind and stop the process.

You will be told some general information about the people who will raise the child. You'll be told roughly what their income is, what is their style of living, their education background, whether or not there are other children. You will never know their name, their address, or any details that would enable you to identify them if you happened to move next door.

Similarly, the adopting parents will know something of you, such as your age, your education and intelligence, the circumstances of your decision to give up the baby and the same general information about the baby's father. They will never know your name or how to find you.

Most adopting parents are open with their children and tell them they are adopted, or chosen. They describe the natural mother in a good light, such as "she really loved you but she was too young to take care of you." It is far better for the child's self-image to say things like this, than to say that the natural mother was an alcoholic with the disposition of a viper, but it does set up images of tender perfection in the child's imagination that the adoptive parents, being flesh and blood, cannot match.

Adopted children often have strong yearnings to find the mother of their fantasy. The urge is particularly acute during periods of adolescent identity-seeking which are critical to emotional maturity. They may feel that by tracing their genetic roots they will know themselves better. Most countries, Canada included, believe this quest is too likely to end in disaster. Adopted children, unlike all other citizens, are not permitted to see their birth registration. Adoption agencies deny access to records.

Finland and Scotland, however, permit adults who were adopted as children to know the names and other identifying information about their natural parents. In 1973, a follow-up study in Scotland indicated that an open records policy is not harmful. Many adopted people expressed relief from the agony of eternal speculation; even when they found their natural parents to be sadly flawed, it was better than wondering.

Once adopted, the child has exactly the same legal position in relation to her adoptive parents as a natural child does. In law she is their child. The adoptive father has the financial responsibility to support the child until she is sixteen, or whatever age applies in that province.

There are so-called private adoptions, arranged usually by doctors who are simultaneously treating one couple for infertility and delivering someone else's unwanted baby. The doctor makes the reasonable decision to solve both problems with a transfer of the baby. Sometimes a couple desiring to adopt a baby learn of someone who is pregnant and doesn't plan to keep the child. They come to a mutual, private agreement to raise the child themselves.

In all cases such adoptions must be administered by a child care agency designated to do so. This provides a necessary protection for the baby and for all the parents involved. The only disadvantage of the private adoption is that confidentiality may not be possible. The adoptive parents are vulnerable to the possibility that the natural mother may turn up on their doorstep in a year or two to claim her child.

In the past, courts took a romantic view of such change-of-hearts and used to respond to blood ties, overlooking the fact that babies bond to whomever takes care of them. Courts used to uproot the child from the familiarity and safety of her only home and award her to the demanding stranger. Happily, with improved awareness of child development needs, this is unlikely to happen today.

*A caution:* some insensitive judges require that the mother who is giving up her child for adoption must identify the baby in court before the final papers are signed. In some cases the mother has never seen the baby and in others she may have had a glimpse of the infant in the delivery room. If this is going to be required of you, brace yourself for one of the most painful experiences of your life: the baby will look wonderful.

Children have been placed for adoption without the consent of the parents when there is evidence that the parents were neglectful or abusive. There is a wide variance in judicial attitude, however. Courts have ruled against such forcible adoptions when the alcoholic father has promised to go on the wagon, even though other brothers and sisters may have been adopted already by the family desiring this child.

In one case where the parents were divorced and the father rarely visited the child, the court would not listen to his attempt to prevent the adoption of that child. In another case the natural father was given time to reform his conduct before the court ruled on his protest.

## You want to adopt a baby

Most agencies will not permit an adoption by an unmarried person, or by two people of the same sex living together. The adoptive parents of choice are married to one another, demonstrate financial and emotional stability, and have not recently given birth to a child.

There are many exceptions. For instance, adoption agencies prefer that the couple be in the age range that corresponds to the child-bearing years of the average marriage, but older people often are permitted to adopt older children. Also, single people are allowed to adopt a child of the same sex in some jurisdictions where adoptive couples are scarce, and someone who has separated from a spouse after the application was made may be allowed to adopt anyway.

It's a supply and demand market. Agencies can be strict in their requirements when couples seek to adopt newborns, since unwed mothers tend to keep their babies these days, but the regulations are relaxed two years later when that same baby is placed for adoption by the overwhelmed parent.

The child care agency will ask you and your spouse to submit to an exhaustive interview and to supply references. The case worker will ask about your marriage and will attempt to learn your husband's true feelings about the proposed adoption. Some men hate the idea but agree reluctantly, an attitude which may emerge later and desolate the child. Some couples whose marriages are in trouble decide to adopt a child "to bring us together". They should see a marriage counsellor together. Babies need wonder-glue, they don't provide it.

Agencies are caring for huge numbers of handicapped children in foster homes and treatment centres. These children are also available for adoption, either singly or in family groups of as many as nine. They present serious problems which should not be minimized, and the agency has a responsibility it should honour to provide back-up services. On the other hand, composed, sensible, affectionate people who have adopted these children and transformed their lives declare sincerely that however beneficial the adoption was for the child concerned, the greater rewards were theirs.

All agencies honour the tradition that children should be adopted by people who have the same religion as the child, or the child's natural mother. In many cases, however, the natural mother does not belong to any denomination or is a member of a religion which does not impose continuity.

Regulations usually require that the adoptive parents must be a minimum of eighteen years older than the child they adopt. Provincial regulations differ slightly, but it is possible to adopt an adult. This kind of adoption sometimes is sought when people want to secure a beloved friend's right to inherit, or when a foster child they have raised wants that extra reassurance. Adults can never be adopted without their consent.

## You do not entirely own your child

Your authority over your child is not unlimited. For instance, you cannot educate your child at home even if you are a qualified teacher: the child must attend school regularly until school-leaving age or you will find yourself in court.

Your rights as a parent can be taken away permanently if you regularly abuse your child, or leave the child untended, or neglect to feed the child. If the child is inordinately filthy, your home may be subjected to an inspection by someone from the health department.

Child care services and family courts used to whisk children out of their homes rather readily. There was, in fact, no other known technique for protecting them. A generation later, with the wrecks of placements in multiple foster homes filling jails and mental hospitals, it was concluded that children—like flowers—suffer when transplanted. It is done now only as a final resort and in the full knowledge that no matter how wonderful the foster home is, the child will be homesick.

Instead child care agencies leave the children with their natural parents and try to protect them by befriending the parents with a warm, supportive, non-rejecting case worker who visits frequently and is on call around the clock.

The agency has the right to pick up any child at any hour, but it must later demonstrate in court that it was justified. The agency cannot keep your child away from you without a court order and you are entitled to retain a lawyer and fight the case. The agency will have a lawyer present arguments for removing the child from your home. The judge will decide between the two points of view, but there is a growing concern that a third lawyer should be present, someone representing the child. It may be that neither your home nor the foster home the agency has in mind is suitable for the child's well-being: something else may be infinitely better.

Family Courts are within the jurisdiction of the provinces so child custody procedure varies across Canada. In general, there is a limited, brief time allowed between removal of a child from the home and a court appearance to explain the action. Rules of evidence are strictly observed in the hearing that follows. Witnesses are sworn to tell the truth and may not give hearsay evidence. Lawyers cross-examine witnesses and, as in adult court, each is supposed to protect the client from being badgered by the other.

Child care workers or the police may take into custody temporarily any child suddenly orphaned, if there is no relative to care for the child, or a child who has been abandoned, a child whose parents are ill, deranged, obviously retarded, or sentenced to prison, children subjected to incest or put out to commit crimes, or children living in an unfit place.

Judges usually keep the options open in these difficult decisions by awarding temporary custody to the agency or a conditional return of the child to the home. The child won't be consulted at all if she is younger than ten. Even if she howls and screams and begs, and many do, the court can never be sure that the child wasn't pressured into the display and will therefore ignore it.

The most severe judgment that a Family Court can make is to award permanent custody to the child care agency. The child becomes a ward of the Crown, whose provincial representative is the Attorney General, and remains so until the age of eighteen. Crown wardship can be extended if the child's situation requires it, such as the cases of physically or mentally handicapped children, but it does not extend beyond the age of twenty-one.

## You can name a guardian

If your child has extensive property or other assets in her own name, you can name an investment advisor as guardian to administer them. This is a special kind of guardianship, which excludes the normal requirement that the guardian have responsibility for the child's care. The guardian does have the duty of ascertaining that the child is receiving proper care and education by you, and must account to the child for all property being managed on her behalf.

When children are in hospital some distance from their homes, or attending school in another country, it may be advisable to appoint someone nearby as a guardian to supervise financial needs or to sign consent for emergency medical procedures.

When parents are under stress, they sometimes wish to have a temporary guardian take over the care of their children. This is done all the time on an informal basis, using grandparents or friends, but isn't as simple if the couple has no other adults in mind. They must appear in Family Court and request an official transfer of custody, which will be granted if it appears to be in the child's best interests. However, they will not be able to get their children back without another court hearing and some evidence of their suitability to resume the parenting role.

## Children of divorce

Two generations ago it was an unvarying rule that when parents were divorced the children belonged to the father. They had his name, they were his financial responsibility, and only he had the earning capacity to support them. Even fathers serving long terms in prison were granted custody of their children.

Then a wave of sentiment about motherhood swept the courts and judges switched dramatically. Younger children almost invariably were awarded to their mothers, the exception being when the father divorced the mother for adultery and established to the court's satisfaction that she was of loose moral character and an unfit mother.

Although there are still judges who hand down arbitrary decisions formed in bleak prejudice, the current mood is more sanguine. Women are seen as capable of economic independence, and therefore able to provide for their children, and men are developing tender parental skills that make it reasonable for them to have custody even of infants, as noted in the 1973 Ontario case of Talsky.

If you and your spouse are in agreement about the custody of the child and how much access each will have, you will not require a judge's ruling. You should have your two lawyers draw up an agreement, however. When signed by you both, it is binding. If it isn't respected you can appeal to the court to enforce it.

But if you are fighting over the children— and nothing is sadder— you must take the dispute to a judge. Divorce is under federal jurisdiction; although practice may vary across the country, generally the courts are consulted only when the children are minors.

The objective is supposed to be the physical, moral, spiritual, emotional and intellectual well-being of the child, but each parent offers some advantages and few cases are clear-cut in favour of one or the other. Adults behave shamefully in most child custody cases. They blacken one another's character in order to lighten their own; they tell exaggerated stories of lewd activities or child neglect. The judge must try to perceive the reality under the stagecraft but, unfortunately, there is rarely any investigation into the family or requests for reports from community agencies.

Usually "children of tender years", that is, under seven, are awarded to the mother. Older boys generally are given into the father's custody and older girls into the mother's. Children older than twelve are asked their preference, a desolating choice for a child to make, and the child's wishes usually are taken into account when the judge reaches a decision. Younger children may be asked into the judge's chambers for a chat, during which the judge makes an attempt to learn the child's true feelings, keeping in mind the likelihood that the parent who has been seeing the child recently has probably tried to influence her.

Finally, having considered more subtleties than the ruling will express, the court comes to a decision and awards custody.

Custody means that one parent now has total authority over the child until she reaches school- and home-leaving age. The court may rule that the parent denied custody can retain jurisdiction over some part of the child's life, such as education, but except in unusual circumstances the parent with custody decides where the child lives, where she goes to school, what she does; the other parent cannot overrule.

There are two elements in a divorce wrangle over children. One is custody and the other is access. With custody decided, the court then deals with the cantankerous issue of how much access the excluded parent will have to visit the child. In cases where the court is persuaded that one parent is dangerous to the well-being of the child, access may be forbidden altogether. Usually the term used is "reasonable access", which often means one day a week and during some vacations.

In one case the court established that as a condition of the father's access to his children, he must not discuss religion with them. In another, where the father hadn't seen his child for four years, the court investigated carefully to determine if the child would be upset by the appearance of a near stranger before allowing the father access.

In another case a mother so upset her child during visits by her criticism of the child's father and siblings that the court ordered her to stop seeing the child. A father was refused access when the child reacted to the sight of him by cringing in terror.

Decisions of a judge concerning custody and access can be appealed but the ruling will not be changed unless it is clear that the judge acted on some wrong principle or disregarded material evidence.

Violation of the court order makes the offender liable to arrest. The parent who has custody, however, can move anywhere in the world, unless there is a restricting court order. It has resulted in the access order becoming meaningless. The parent with access is not permitted to keep the child beyond the stipulated period, but well-to-do parents have been known to kidnap their children and keep them for years while the courts maunder over the case.

## Control of the child

In general, the law takes the view that the parents, especially the father, have the right to restrain and control the acts of their children and to punish them for disobedience. This right to strike a child applies only to minors. Parents may not hit or confine children older than sixteen to eighteen (depending on the provincial age of consent).

The law leaves the method of correction to the parent's discretion. It is legal to hit even a small child with sticks, leather belts or fists. So long as no one reports the abuse, or the child is not so injured as to require hospitalization, or has not been sexually molested, there will be no interference.

School teachers and others acting in a parental role, such as summer camp supervisors and Girl Guide leaders on an outing, can hit a child. The instrument used and the amount of pain inflicted are supposed to be "reasonable".

Many people believe that hitting a child frequently will improve the child's character, despite all the evidence that the most violent, anti-social people in our society were beaten regularly as children. If you do not want your child to be struck by other adults, such as a teacher, you should advise them accordingly. However, you can be ignored.

## Your child breaks the law

Are you responsible? Yes, if the child has been skipping school, or is on the street in the middle of the night. You can be taken to court and fined. The law can even send you to prison for persistent violations of truancy or curfew laws, or move to take custody of the children away from you. If your child steals or vandalizes property, you may be asked to make reparation.

Parents used to have the right to send to jail any of their children they didn't particularly like. The child would be described as "incorrigible", which in the case of boys usually meant that they were unruly and in the case of girls that they were sexually active. The children would then be confined behind bars for indefinite sentences which went on for years.

Ontario stopped permitting this sanctioned child abuse in 1975, and other provinces are moving in the same direction. When parents are in serious conflict with a child, it is beginning to be seen as a social problem requiring help for the whole family rather than the punishing of the "bad" child.

# 4  All about sex

Despite the Prime Minister's declaration that the law has no business in the bedrooms of the nation, the fact is that the law is omnipresent under the bedclothes. The law controls the availability of contraceptives, takes an interest in your sexual activities when deciding whether or not you are worthy of welfare or alimony, and even pays perky attention to your sexual experiments. There are certain sexual acts, anal-genital for instance, which are grounds for divorce. And one man went from court to court, appealing a heavy sentence in prison, before he at last encountered a judge who didn't think that oral-genital sex was a threat to social order.

## Obscenity

The definition of obscenity in Canadian criminal law is "undue exploitation of sex", which is no definition at all unless there is agreement on what is undue. The law is therefore a moving object: it depends on public taste, which is always changing.

It depends for its enforcement, however, on police taste which generally is not out on the leading edge of change.

The Law Reform Commission of Canada, in *Working Paper 10*, examines obscenity, and worries, quite rightly, on the effect of obscenity on the minds of children whose attitudes are not yet formed and of the brutalizing element in scenes of sado-masochistic sex. But it wonders if what it terms private obscenity— that is, books, films, plays that are clearly designated as containing pornography— offers any threat to society.

The paper comments, "'It takes all sorts to make a world' is more than a plea for tolerance— it is a tribute to the virtue of variety. To this variety individual freedom is essential."

Individual freedom should be curtailed only in the area of public obscenity, the Law Reform Commission suggested—billboards, store-window displays, media with a general audience circulation, and

52   The Law is not for Women

the like, which it termed a form of public menace nuisance. But, except in circumstances where children were exposed to it, "private obscenity in our view should no longer be a crime."

In the meantime obscenity laws on the books are being enforced unevenly across the country. Clerks in bookstores have been arrested and manacled in recent years; art galleries have been closed down; a theatre group was barred from further performances of a spoof on pornography.

## Sex underage

No person may involve a child under the age of fourteen in a sexual act, even with the child's consent, even at the child's instigation. It is not a defence if the child claimed to be older or appeared to be older. If the adult in the relationship has authority over the child, the child can't in law give consent until he or she is sixteen.

## Rape

The law has been slightly improved. Until recently, all rape trials were trials of the victim rather than the rapist. Unless she had been a virgin and was left half dead, the atmosphere of the courtroom was heavy with the suggestion that the victim had lured the poor man and that she really enjoyed the encounter.

Judges were required to tell the jury that the testimony of the victim was not sufficient to bring in a verdict of guilty: there had to be corroborating witnesses as well. Unlike any other crime in Canadian jurisprudence, the sworn testimony of the victim was considered doubtful evidence. It was as though someone who had been mugged was not believed in court and had to prove that the mugging wasn't invited.

An amendment to the Criminal Code has removed this necessity for corroborating evidence but the laws concerning rape are still unsatisfactory. In June 1975, the Minister of Justice was criticized for the clauses in the new legislation which cloak rape trials in secrecy, providing for anonymity of the victim and a change of city for the hearing. The suggestion reinforced the air of shame that already infects attitudes about victims of rape—that their identity would need to be protected because they are dishonoured. Women's organizations have been pressing to have the charge of rape removed from the Criminal Code and the crime itself treated as an act of physical assault, devoid of the special treatment given rapists.

Further, the new legislation retained the concept that women who imply consent cannot be raped. This leads to humiliating examinations of the woman's sexual experience. If she could not prove that she had a "previously chaste character", the law denies her the right to say no to any man.

Women who testify against their assailants in rape trials have been asked if they are on the pill, if they have ever been pregnant, if they have had an abortion, if they have had a venereal disease, at what age did they lose their virginity, how many sexual partners have they had, if they smoke marijuana, if they took drugs, how much they enjoy sex, do they have orgasms.

"Is it any wonder rape is the least reported of all crimes and therefore the most successful because the victim does not complain?" asked Mr. Justice E.L. Haines of the Supreme Court of Ontario in an article in Chitty's Law Journal. "Indeed in this second ordeal the victim may be compelled under oath to destroy herself."

Some judges have moved to protect rape victims in the courtroom. The Saskatchewan Court of Appeal in 1974 limited the admissability of evidence of the victim's previous personal life. In commenting on it at a later trial, Mr. Justice R.A. MacDonald said, "It is not this woman who is on trial."

At present, the penalties for people convicted of rape are so severe that juries flinch from finding the accused guilty. There is a possible life sentence for forcible rape. Statutory rape, which is the term applied to all sexual relations with persons underage, is punishable by a life sentence when the partner was younger than fourteen, and five years when the sexual act took place between an adult in a position of authority and someone of fifteen or sixteen years of age.

A wife cannot charge her husband with rape. The marriage contract permits him unlimited sexual access.

Rape describes penetration of a woman's vagina by the male's penis. When men force women into acts of oral or anal sex, the offense is called sexual assault.

Because women cringe from the inquisition they must face, very few even report sexual attacks and fewer still are willing to lay a charge. In 1971 there were only 119 people charged with rape in Canada; 54 were acquitted.

Rape cases usually are tried by all-male juries. Lawyers believe that women jurors would be unduly sympathetic to the victim; they do not apply the same logic to the possible bias of male jurors towards the accused.

If you are raped and your inclination is to have the man arrested, you must report the attack at once. Do not wash or clean yourself up in any way. Go to a hospital and insist on a physical examination to obtain semen samples and have a record of marks or other injuries. You will be required to demonstrate to the police that you protested; even if a knife was held to your throat, you are expected to scream and have witnesses to prove it.

There are at least eight Rape Crisis Centres in Canada and more springing up all the time. Two are in Vancouver and the others in Toronto, Ottawa, Montreal, Calgary, Saskatoon and Swift Current. They are not going to pressure you one way or the other about reporting the attack or laying charges. They will provide information about your alternatives and, best of all, comfort you for your shakes and feelings of disgrace and self-disgust.

Some police departments are discouraging their officers from bullying women who have been raped. None have so far followed the lead of the New York City police department in setting up specially trained squads to respond to rape crimes.

The Women's Bureau of the Ontario Ministry of Labour, Women of Unifarm in Alberta, the YWCA Women's Centre in Montreal, and many other organizations concerned with women's rights have printed instructions available for victims of rape. They emphasize that if you report the crime you should have some supportive person with you. Police are less likely to make lewd remarks in the presence of a witness.


## Other sexual offences

It is against the law for a man to have sexual relations with a woman who is mentally retarded or insane, and therefore incapable of giving assent responsibly. It is not against the law, curiously, for a woman to have sexual relations with a mentally retarded or insane man.

A man may not have sexual intercourse with his stepdaughter, foster daughter or female ward under the age of sixteen, or with a woman employee of "previously chaste character" under the age of twenty-one. There is no law against women having sexual relations with stepsons, foster sons, male wards or male employees of any age, chaste or otherwise.

A man may not seduce a woman who is between the ages of sixteen and eighteen if her character was "previously chaste". He is punishable by a prison sentence of up to two years. There is no reference in the law to women seducing males of this age group.

55   All about sex

A man older than twenty-one cannot promise to marry a woman "of previously chaste character" in order to win his way into her bed. The judge will let him off if he marries her, but otherwise he could serve a sentence of two years. There is no provision in law prohibiting women from seducing males with a promise to marry them.

It is against the law for a woman passenger on a boat to be seduced by the captain, the owner, or a member of the crew. The offender must marry the woman in order to avoid arrest. Women who own boats can seduce male passengers with impunity.

There are sentences of up to five years for what are described vaguely by the Criminal Code as "acts of gross indecency" between people who are not married, not both older than twenty-one, or not both consenting. The definition of gross indecency is left up to the sophistication of the arresting officers and the judge. In some parts of the country, oral-genital sex is considered depraved.

Buggery, which is anal intercourse between humans, is punishable by sentences of up to fourteen years if one of the participants is not willing or is under the age of twenty-one. Bestiality, intercourse with an animal, is punishable by the same sentence.

Sexual activity must be private. You cannot do it in the road. It is an indecent act to copulate in a public place, or in the presence of others— which means that group sex is illegal— or to have sexual intercourse anywhere where the intent is to insult or offend.

The term "consenting adults" means that there has been no use of force, threats, or fear of bodily harm used in order to gain the cooperation of the partner. The partner must not be feeble-minded, insane, or drugged.

You cannot be nude in a public place, or on your own property where you are not screened from public view.

You can't expose your genitals or your breasts in a public place. This law is not usually enforced in bars, body-rub parlors or discothèques; it is enforced on most summer beaches in Canada, however.

Men who are parents or guardians are liable for sentences of up to fourteen years if they pimp for females under the age of fourteen who are in their care, or if they accept money that the child has obtained by sexual activity. If the young person in their custody is older than fourteen, the sentence is a maximum of five years.

There is no law prohibiting a parenting woman from living off the prostitution of a male child in her family.

The law views sexual intercourse as penile penetration "to even the slightest degree, notwithstanding that seed is not emitted." For that reason sexual intercourse between two women is a legal impossibility.

# Homosexuality

There is no law against homosexual acts so long as sexual intercourse takes place in private between no more than two consenting adults. A charge of gross indecency can be laid at the discretion of the police if the sexual act takes place with an audience. A gay bar, public washroom, or secluded nook in a park is not considered a private place.

Human rights legislation does not forbid discrimination against homosexuals. Homosexuals have been fired explicitly because of their sexual preference and have been unable to find sufficient support for reinstatement. Homosexuals can be refused employment everywhere, and especially by the government. A homosexual parent can have her child taken into custody because her sexuality makes her an unfit parent.

There are strict laws concerning sexual relations between men and vulnerable women, such as those who are underage or dependent upon the male. But there are no laws to protect vulnerable women from sexual advances by women in positions of authority or seniority.

There is a law against one man attacking another with the intention to commit buggery. It is called assault, not rape. Presumably a woman who is sexually attacked by another woman could also lay a charge of assault rather than rape, since rape is a heterosexual act by legal definition.

Homosexuals have been married to one another by clergy, but the union is not a marriage in the legal sense and neither is under any financial obligation with respect to the other. The couple can draw up a contract, however, which will establish division of property in the event of a separation. A will protects right of inheritance. Both documents require a lawyer's advice.

In December 1974 a Manitoba judge ruled that two men who had been married by a Unitarian minister were not married in the legal sense. The judge turned down their request for a court order to have the marriage registered, admitting that neither Parliament nor the Manitoba legislature expressly forbids marriages between people of the same sex but interpreting the phrase "any two persons" in the provincial Marriage Act to mean one of each gender. It is an interpretation that probably will be tested in the Supreme Court of Canada some day.

# Incest

Sexual intercourse with someone known to be a blood relative, such as a parent, child, brother, sister, half-brother, half-sister, grandparent or grandchild, is called incest. Incest is punishable by prison terms of up to fourteen years.

To avoid prosecution, women involved in an incestuous relationship must prove that they did so under duress. A man cannot avoid prosecution by making the same claim against his mother, sister, half-sister or grandmother.

## Prostitution

There is no law against prostitution but there is a new amendment to the Criminal Code which prohibits men or women from soliciting in a public place with a view to selling sexual services. The method of apprehending the prostitute is often entrapment: the police officer hangs out where prostitutes are known to congregate and behaves as men do when hoping to make a contact. The person who then approaches him is arrested for soliciting.

Customers of prostitutes are not arrested unless they happen to be caught in a raid on a bawdy house. One woman judge in California who insisted on dismissing all charges against prostitutes because there were no similar charges against their customers was removed from that courtroom.

Anyone who runs a bawdy house, which is the legal description of a house of prostitution, is committing an offence. Anyone who lives on the proceeds of prostitution, even partly, is liable for a prison sentence of up to ten years.

# 5 All about abortion

Abortion has become the most divisive issue that Canada has known since the bitterness of the conscription debate during World War II. It is not a resolvable argument, since both sides claim to be morally right.

Opponents of abortion believe that the operation kills a human being and is therefore murder. Certainly a society which has a callous regard for life is debased and coarsened, but those who advocate the removal of laws restricting abortion also speak of concern for a human life, the woman's. Motherhood, they say, should not be forced on the unwilling or unready.

In the 1940s the Prime Minister of Canada, William Lyon Mackenzie King, avoided confronting the passionate controversy over conscription by declaring his firm policy: "Conscription if necessary, but not necessarily conscription." No one knew what he meant, but the ambiguity of the government's position kept potential rioters at home. The same state of baffling compromise has been exercised in the question of abortion. Canada both has legal abortion available from coast to coast and it hasn't.

In 1969 the Criminal Code was amended by Parliament to allow doctors to perform therapeutic abortions without fear of arrest, provided they follow the stringent conditions outlined in the legislation. The continuation of a pregnancy must be shown to be "likely to endanger her life or health." "Health" is almost meaningless in the medical sense; it is often interpreted broadly to include the concept of "a state of well-being", a formula which would stretch to cover even dismay at being pregnant.

This adjustment in the legal wording was accompanied by a number of other conditions which must be met for a legal abortion. A doctor who agrees to perform an abortion can carry out the procedure only in a hospital approved by the Canadian Council on Hospital Accreditation and only if the doctor has obtained permission from a Therapeutic Abortion Committee composed of not fewer than three doctors appointed by the hospital board.

These abortion regulations are permissive, not mandatory. Hospitals retain their feudal autonomy and can either opt into the legislation or behave as though it didn't exist. Most Canadian hospitals have chosen the latter course. In 1974 the Canadian Medical Association Journal reported that only 259 hospitals of the 1,359 accredited in Canada had abortion committees. That splinter group decreases every year. In 1975 there were only 254 accredited hospitals. The sharpest decline was in Quebec, which went from thirty-one hospitals to twenty-seven; the other hospital to drop out was in Newfoundland.

The law neither obliges hospitals to establish abortion committees nor requires that such committees approve abortions at all. Some hospitals have committees which almost never meet: at other hospitals, there is a weekly quota, which can be adjusted according to the vagaries of the political climate.

Abortion committees can invent whatever machinery the hospital wishes. Some rule that applications must be made by two doctors, not one, and that one must be a psychiatrist. At least one hospital also insists that every applicant submit to an interview with a social worker, who then reports to the committee, which is chaired by a doctor who disapproves of abortion.

Hospitals with active Therapeutic Abortion Committees are under pressure to cut back or cease approving abortions entirely. Since 1973 much of this opposition has taken the form of anti-abortion groups joining hospital associations in overnight membership blitzes in order to gain control of the hospital's Board of Directors.

Some of the pressure came from the then Justice Minister Otto Lang. In 1974 he sent some hospitals a memorandum complaining about "too relaxed an interpretation" of the definition of "health". He warned that he had spoken to provincial Attorneys General to suggest "a tightening up of the way in which the law is being interpreted".

Subsequently, a number of hospitals nervously did reduce the quota of abortions the committees approved. One of these, Scarborough Centenary Hospital on the outskirts of Toronto, performed 975 therapeutic abortions in 1973 and 750 in 1974.

A breakdown of Scarborough Centenary's abortion cases corresponds roughly to the situations behind the some 40,000 therapeutic abortions performed in Canada in 1974. Almost half, forty-two per cent, involved women twenty years old and younger; fifty-five per cent were performed on women between the ages of twenty-one and forty; three per cent of the women were older than forty. Single women made up fifty-five per cent of the cases, married women thirty-five per cent, separated or divorced women ten per cent.

Scarborough Centenary noted the religion of the patients in only eighty-two consecutive cases: of these forty-two were of Protestant denominations, thirty-one were Roman Catholics and the rest of other faiths or none. That same ratio has been noted across the country.

Between five and seven per cent of the abortions performed in the hospital involved women made pregnant by rape.

Across Canada it has been noted that almost half the therapeutic abortions are performed on teenagers. It is part of the trend towards increased evidence of adolescent despair: more teen-age suicides, more teen-agers in trouble with the law, more teen-agers coming into custody of child care agencies, more teen-agers with severe emotional problems. Teen-agers who become pregnant are part of this larger problem of vulnerable, rootless young people. Thirteen-year-olds are having abortions in Canada and thirteen-year-olds are having babies. Either way, it's a human tragedy.

At best, abortion is a desperate and sad last resort. It presents the caring professions with a dilemma. On the one hand, there is deep-rooted medical training which stresses the preservation of life— and fetal tissue at twelve weeks is recognizably human— and on the other, concern for the frantic, shocked woman who isn't ready for motherhood.

The Canadian Medical Association has asked the government to repeal abortion legislation and allow women and their doctors to decide the matter for themselves, according to their individual consciences. The government has declared that the legislation is non-negotiable for some time to come.

In the meantime, it *is* possible to obtain a legal abortion in Canada. The major factors to be considered are timing and geography.

## Step one

*Maybe you are not pregnant.* Menstrual periods are capricious. Under the stress of knowing that you were unprotected during sexual intercourse, you might have a late period or miss it altogether. Panic is particularly common among teen-agers, whose menstrual cycles can be uneven in normal circumstances.

On the other hand, maybe you are. Even if you have been using a contraceptive, it is not impossible to become pregnant. The pill is the most reliable of all contraceptives but skipping even one day can destroy its effectiveness. Even sterilization can fail: tubal ligations have been botched, and there is a brief period after a vasectomy when semen may contain sperm.

Of the 903 women who sought abortions in Ottawa through the counselling services offered by ARCAL (71 Bank Street, (613) 232-9606) in 1973, 282 reported that they had been using some method of birth control. One-third had relied on rhythm; another large group depended on foam, condoms and I.U.D.s; three had undergone tubal ligations, and two had mated with men who had vasectomies.

The point is: find out from a doctor whether or not you are pregnant. Don't guess and procrastinate and fret.

You need a gynecologist, obstetrician, or family practitioner. If you decide you will be asking for an abortion if the doctor finds you pregnant, you'd better start out with a doctor who is sympathetic. This is the key, but how are you to know?

Ask women's organizations of the feminist persuasion. If there is a centre offering birth control counselling, the staff almost certainly knows which doctors in town will help you. In some cities the YWCA fills this role; public health nurses are often a good resource; so are child care agency social workers, many of whom have strong feelings about the adverse effects of children born to unwilling mothers.

Or you can look up doctors in your telephone directory Yellow Pages. It may be agony for you if you are shy and inexperienced but you have a perfect right to ask whoever answers the doctor's phone whether or not the doctor will agree to terminate your pregnancy, if it turns out after the examination that you are pregnant. If not, will the nurse or doctor kindly direct you to someone who will?

Doctors function under a code of ethics which allows them to refuse to perform an abortion but requires that they must refer these cases when asked to a qualified person who will do so. Any doctor who refuses to refer you should be reported at once to the Canadian Medical Association, 1867 Alta Vista Drive, Ottawa, or to the provincial disciplinary body, the College of Physicians and Surgeons.

There is another slower and more devious route. You can contact your local hospital to determine if it has an active Therapeutic Abortion Committee. *Active* is an important part of your inquiry. Some hospital abortion committees almost never approve abortions: one, for instance, does so only when the applicant has six living children. There is no point in contacting a Roman Catholic hospital, but non-denominational or Jewish teaching hospitals linked to universities often have abortion committees.

Geography is a crucial factor. British Columbia, which has only one-third of Quebec's population, has nearly twice as many hospitals with active abortion committees: fifty-two. The distribution varies within provinces: for instance, Sudbury in northern Ontario has no facilities for abortions, while Toronto and Hamilton have a cluster of hospitals which will terminate pregnancies.

It should take only a simple call to the hospital's information centre in order to find out whether or not there is an abortion committee. For some incomprehensible reason, most hospitals try to conceal this information from the public. You should ask to speak to the gynecology out-patient department or the gynecology floor. The nurse or receptionist who answers may give you the information and tell you whether the hospital's policy is restrictive or not. You will almost certainly not be given the name of a doctor who will help you, unless the nurse or receptionist sticks her neck out and violates the rules.

Your next step is to locate a doctor with privileges in that hospital, but not one who sits on the abortion committee. Doctors on abortion committees are disqualified by law from referring patients for abortions. Try a visit to the out-patient department. One desperate woman hung around, introducing herself and her problem to everyone wearing a white jacket until she was told the name of a doctor who would help her. It seems a silly and humiliating way to get legitimate information about a health service.

There may be an Academy of Medicine office in your community. It is set up to provide the name and telephone number of doctors who are on call in emergencies. Explain your emergency and trust that the Academy of Medicine respects the official view of the Canadian Medical Association that abortions should not be this difficult to obtain.

If you live in a part of the country where hospitals refuse to establish abortion committees, you will need money to travel. Contact by telephone or mail the women's centre in whatever city is nearest you and the staff will make the appointments for you. In Vancouver, for instance, Women's Liberation is at (604) 684-0523; in Montreal Women's Liberation is at (514) 844-5838; in Toronto try CARES (Central Abortion Referral and Education Services) at (416) 921-2151.

Perhaps you will have to go to the United States, which means your medical and hospitalization insurance won't cover you. It is more expensive, and less safe for you, if you delay. The United States, however, offers a procedure rarely done in Canada: it is called menstrual extraction, which means what it seems to mean. It is a method of starting your period when you are only a week or two late, when it is too soon for tests to detect whether or not you actually are pregnant.

## Step two

At least one Canadian hospital, Vancouver General, is approving almost all applications for abortion. Most hospitals, however, reject about a third of all requests, usually turning down women whose pregnancy is beyond the first three months and women from out-of-town. To avoid the latter you should obtain the address of a friend or sympathetic stranger who lives in the hospital's catchment area and use it as your own.

Which leaves the problem of delay. If you are certain that you do not wish to continue your pregnancy, you have only six weeks in which to find the doctor and the hospital where the abortion can be done; pregnancy cannot be verified until about six weeks after conception and most hospitals refuse to perform abortions after the twelfth week. Besides, therapeutic abortions are safer and much less traumatic emotionally when they are done within the first three months.

At this point in the pregnancy the method known as apiration or vacuum can be used, usually accompanied by a mild amount of curettage. Both require dilatation of the cervix, which is done under a light anaesthetic, usually a "ring block", which is preceded by something from the tranquilizing family to help you relax.

The procedure is done on an out-patient basis regularly in the United States and never in Canada, except by Dr. Henry Morgentaler of Montreal who was sent to prison because he did not perform abortions in a hospital. Some Canadian hospitals require patients for therapeutic abortions to spend two nights in hospital, the night before the operation and the night after.

Your doctor may insert some packing in your cervix the day before the operation in order to begin dilatation. This will result in strong cramps, like those you may have experienced in menstrual periods. If you are not forewarned, these can be alarming.

Pregnancies which have advanced to the fourth month or more will only be terminated if there are special circumstances, such as the delay not being your fault and your situation one that gives real concern for your mental state. The abortion technique commonly used at this point is saline injection. Depending on how advanced the pregnancy is, the doctor may decide to perform a hysterotomy. This is similar to a caesarian section and involves an abdominal incision and a longer recuperative period in hospital.

## Step three: after the abortion

Make certain you will never again have a pregnancy you don't want. Consult a doctor to obtain the contraceptive pill or device that suits your needs and use it, without fail. Unless you and your partner are responsible and consistent about the contraceptive of your choice, you are almost certain to be pregnant again. Doctors and abortion committees understandably are distressed when women return for a second and even a third abortion because they can't be bothered with contraceptives. Some hospitals refuse to perform the third abortion unless the woman consents to be sterilized at the same time.

Birth control pills aren't the perfect contraceptive but, taken as directed, they are the best method around today. Diaphragms and I.U.D.s work for many women, and so do condoms, especially when used in conjunction with spermicide jelly or foam. Rhythm and withdrawal are both high-wire acts.

The doctor who performs the abortion will advise on contraceptives, or else direct you to someone who will.

Every woman who is sexually active should have birth control counselling. This especially includes those dreamy romantics who have intercourse for the first time without protection and afterwards consider themselves somehow immune to their biological functions, and those oddballs who believe that there is something cold-blooded about premeditated protection.

A girl younger than home-leaving age is in a delicate legal position. (See: *You and doctors*, page 3). If communication in the home doesn't allow confiding in the parents, it might be advisable for the girl to ask for help in a women's centre or birth control counselling agency without mentioning her age.

The best organized resources for birth control and abortion counselling are the branches of the Family Planning Federation of Canada. A list of their locations is given in the Appendix on page 151.

## Hazards of abortion

A therapeutic abortion in Canada is safer than childbirth. Fifty-four women died of childbirth and complications of pregnancy in Canada in 1972, while none died of legal abortions. In that year, however, one woman is known to have died of an illegal abortion in Quebec.

There is argument as to whether women are more likely to suffer severe depression because they have been refused an abortion or because they have just had one. Depending on the viewpoint of the research team, either can be demonstrated. It is clear, however, that the likelihood of emotional distress increases when the abortion is delayed.

The controversy about the necessity for children to be wanted in order to assure them of perfect bliss is also flawed. Extremely unhappy, desolate women often want their babies with every fibre of their beings. They expect that the baby will provide them with warmth and approval, which babies do not do—especially when their care is inadequate. Studies of battered babies demonstrate that most of them were wanted.

On the other hand, it can be shown that babies suffer when born too close together, or when they are raised by an exhausted mother or a resentful one.

## Alternatives

Some women are in the ideal position of being absolutely clear how they feel about abortion: they are either unalterably opposed or else can accept it. The ones in pain are those in the middle, torn between their feelings of maternal tenderness and curiosity and the distress of the pregnancy's untimeliness. They hang in indecision, bombarded by impulses, a situation which frequently results in delay. The delay becomes the decision-maker: the woman puts it off until she cannot obtain an abortion.

Women who are unsure of their course should seek advice from a respected source. People who are trying to make up their minds on some matter usually already have on an unconscious level. They tend to shop around waiting for the echo to the decision they have already made, consulting a succession of people until someone gets it right. Inner voices have a lot of moxie and often know more about you than you do.

Unmarried women are under a good deal of pressure usually to marry. This is a high-risk solution, particularly when the woman is in her teens. Unions which take place because a baby is on the way are failure-prone; when they collapse, as the majority do, three lives have been damaged. There is evidence that the baby pays the highest penalty: Robert Shaw, director of Dellcrest treatment centre in Toronto for emotionally disturbed children, once reported that a high proportion of his patients were born of shotgun marriages.

Adoption is an alternative to abortion, forced marriage, or unreadiness to raise a child. Children's Aid Societies, Family Service Associations, members of the clergy, birth control counsellors and Right to Life groups can give information and guidance. There will be no difficulty finding a welcoming home for your infant.

Unmarried women often reject abortion or adoption and opt for raising their baby themselves, a decision which is becoming so common that there is much less social stigma attached to her or the child. If this is your plan, you should take into account your financial resources. Without support from your family or the baby's father it will be necessary for you to work, which means finding a day care centre that takes infants, or else you will have to live on welfare payments.

In Canada welfare payments for a woman and baby are considerably less than the old age pension that a couple receives, which is itself inadequate for more than a scrimping existence. You and your child will have a thin time of it: unless you can get subsidized housing you will have real difficulty in having enough left over from your rent payments to feed either of you adequately, and your baby's future health and intelligence are dependent on a high-quality diet in the first eighteen months of life.

Your baby must also receive consistent affectionate care, someone who will bond with the baby during the critical first six months, someone who will play with her, touch her and talk to her so that she will develop a basis of confidence and enthusiasm. A makeshift arrangement of irregular, overworked baby-sitters will result in an unhappy, confused, discouraged infant.

Some cities are developing co-op housing for single mothers where they can pool supervision of the babies while pursuing on a part-time basis their careers, job training, or education upgrading courses. Consult child care agencies, women's groups, hospital social workers, welfare offices or public health nurses.

## Age limit

Despite the unwillingness of most doctors to deal with young underage patients without the knowledge of parents, some hospitals are chance-takers in some situations. The Hospital for Sick Children in Toronto, for instance, in rare circumstances will provide sexually active teenagers with contraceptives. A few hospitals will treat venereal disease on an out-patient basis, in their clinics, without challenging teen-agers who give their age as "eighteen". Abortion is surgery, however, and will not be performed on minors without written consent from parents or legal guardians.

## About illegal abortions

A fully qualified doctor who performs a medically safe abortion on a woman without the consent of a therapeutic abortion committee in an accredited hospital is breaking the law, and so is the patient. Section 251 of the Criminal Code states that "everyone" who seeks "the miscarriage of a female person, whether she is pregnant or not . . . is guilty of an indictable offense and liable to imprisonment for life." The woman can be sent to prison for up to two years.

A few doctors are running this risk. In the wake of Dr. Henry Morgentaler's imprisonment in 1975, more than a hundred Quebec doctors indicated support for him by declaring that they too had performed abortions outside of the legal regulations.

Women who obtain illegal abortions from qualified physicians are probably in no danger of losing their lives but they are breaking the law and they risk arrest, along with the doctor. Even so, if you feel it is imperative to terminate your pregnancy, and if you have no access in your community to legal abortion, it is advisable to find a doctor who is willing to break the law.

Under no circumstances should you seek an abortion from anyone but a qualified doctor. The procedures used by backroom abortionists are painful and dangerous. You can become infected or be mutilated so that you will never be able to have a child. There is a very good risk that you may be killed.

# 6 All about separation

Some separations involve couples who can agree, without being acquisitive or vindictive, how the property will be divided. If you are financially self-sufficient, or intend to be, there may not be any need for support from your husband. He is legally obliged to help support his children, but you may be able to agree amicably to share this expense on some basis proportionate to your incomes.

Such separations can be done verbally. If later on you decide that you want alimony after all, or if help with the children's support is not forthcoming, you can sue your estranged husband in provincial Supreme Court for alimony or take him to Family Court for child support payments. You may get nowhere with an alimony suit unless you can prove that your husband deserted you, or that he has a steady adulterous relationship, or that he has mistreated you in such a way as to be described in law as cruelty.

Even if one or all of the above is true, your suit will fail if your husband can prove that you are living with another man.

All of this applies when you want to be separated but do not want a divorce. If you decide to divorce your husband you can be awarded alimony on an interim basis while the case is pending.

In Quebec separation agreements are illegal. The Civil Code of that province states that married people are bound to live together; your husband must permit you to live with him wherever he is and you cannot agree otherwise. If you want to live apart without divorcing you must prove in court that your husband refuses to allow you to live with him, or that he has committed adultery, or that he doesn't support you, or that he is cruel. You have no right to live apart from your husband until the court rules that you have proved just cause. Quebec women are urged to see a lawyer *before* leaving their husbands; it is probably a good idea for any woman planning to instigate marriage break-up to consult a lawyer first.

In other provinces mutual agreement to separate is often done on an informal basis. Lawyers enter the picture only when disputes arise about property, children, or support payments.

There is a tendency for the spouse who presses for the separation to feel guilty and make generous concessions, which may later be regretted. Couples normally are so dazed with the misery of break-up that neither is in a mood to be analytical about the division of property. One woman sorting the record collection was so distraught at the memories it evoked that she told her husband to take it all.

Splendid gestures are great theatre but they can have sickening aftermaths. A separation agreement establishing areas of responsibility and ownership of property is a binding legal document that will clarify the muddle of good will and recriminations. If a separation agreement is breached, the offender can be hauled into court.

The court then examines sharply the state of your marriage before the separation agreement. The judge must be assured that the marriage really did break down and that this is not a case of a couple attempting to gain income tax benefits. If the separation agreement puts one spouse at a serious disadvantage, the judge may invalidate it and order a new one.

The courts cannot order you to separate and they can't demand that you reconcile your disagreement. Neither can one spouse force the other to enter into a separation agreement unwillingly. And you must really have separated: if you continue to see one another in a friendly way and have sexual relations, you are married, you are not separated.

Watch out for the *dum casta* clause. It is compulsory chastity. If your husband's lawyer slips in the *dum casta* clause, you forfeit all your rights if you have sexual relations with another man. As has been noted elsewhere in this book, in law a wife's sexual apparatus belongs exclusively to her husband if he is supporting her; if one stops, so does the other.

Your husband's lawyer will want the *dum casta* clause in the agreement, even if your husband is appalled at the idea of locking you in a chastity belt. Lawyers cite the unhappy precedent of a woman whose separation agreement omitted *dum casta* and who demanded her alimony even after she subsequently was divorced and remarried. The first husband had to take the matter to court in order to be freed of the obligation.

You can put in a *dum casta* clause of your own, requiring that your husband "remain true" or else jeopardize the separation agreement.

These sexual restrictions, however, are no longer interpreted as meaning a one-night encounter. In order to dissolve the separation agreement in which they are contained, there must be proof in court that there is a long-standing relationship with a third person.

Your husband's lawyer may also insert a clause which will contract you out of the claim to your estranged husband's estate if he dies without leaving a valid will. Exclusion clauses stand up in court only when worded with considerable finesse. If the financial arrangement in your separation agreement was the payment of a lump sum, which you have received, the court probably would not grant you any further claim to the estate. If you have been receiving regular fixed payments, a court likely will order that they be continued by the administrators of the estate.

If you have property, you may wish to exclude your estranged husband from inheriting same. It makes for less confusion, however, if you simply draw up a new will.

Separation agreements usually contain promises by both parties that they will not "molest, annoy or interfere" with one another. This is the anti-vengeance machinery; even if you are both co-operating magnificently it is wise to include this provision.

Custody of children is an important part of separation agreements. You must state which parent has the custody (equally shared custody is a legal rarity, but may not be impossible) and how access will be provided to the other parent. Financial responsibility for the children is also decided in the agreement. The father customarily bears this alone but if you are employed this burden is shared. It is a good idea these days to work out contingency plans for such situations as you becoming employed or needing education upgrading or job training.

Your home is part of the separation agreement, which must establish not only which spouse will live in it but who is responsible for mortgage and tax payments. Your dower right to one-third the value of the home is now on shaky ground. You may have lost it if you insisted on the separation, if you walked out on him, or if you are living with another man.

You have no automatic right to remain in the home unless you are celibate, and your husband deserted you, treated you cruelly, or is living with another woman. If you can prove your chastity and his lapses, you are allowed to stay in the house and lock him out. Otherwise the house is his and he can return at will. The law will allow you to stay in the house more readily if you are suing for divorce rather than stopping at separation.

You can continue to use your husband's credit to purchase necessities such as food, clothing, and shelter for you and the children, providing that you do not exceed the price range that your husband has established and providing that the separation is *entirely* his idea and you are living a blameless celibate life. If you have agreed together to separate, you may not use his credit.

You own nothing if you have not been earning some income outside your home. If you have been an unpaid housewife, everything you purchased with his money is his. The money you may have saved from your housekeeping allowance is also his, even if you put it in a bank in your name or bought stocks in your own name.

If you both worked during the marriage the situation may be different. It often happens, however, that the woman's income goes on such consumables as foods and vacations, freeing the man's income for hardware such as mortgage and car payments. When that happens he has receipts which establish his ownership and she has nothing.

# SAMPLE SEPARATION AGREEMENT

Here is a sample separation agreement drawn up by a couple with a house, a car and two small children:

THIS SEPARATION AGREEMENT made April 3, 1976,
BETWEEN:

JOHN RICHARD DOE

— and—

JANE LOUISE DOE

WITNESSES:

The parties were married to each other in the City of ... in the Province of ... on June 2, 1969. Throughout this agreement they are called respectively the "husband" and the "wife". In the event the marriage is dissolved the terms shall be construed to mean "former husband" and "former wife". The husband and wife have two children, Richard Peter Doe born August 18, 1970, and Carolyn Jane Doe born February 12, 1973; both of whom are collectively called the "children" throughout, and each of whom is individually called the "child" throughout.

As a result of irreconcilable differences between them, the husband and the wife have been living separate and apart since September 13, 1975, and each of them desires to settle by agreement all rights, claims, demands and causes of action which each has or may have against the other with respect to their property and with respect to any rights either or each of them has, or may have to alimony, maintenance or support from the other.

THEREFORE, the husband and wife agree and acknowledge as follows:

1.  LIVING SEPARATE AND APART: The husband and wife will continue to live separate and apart from each other for the rest of their lives.

2. **FREEDOM FROM THE OTHER:** Neither husband nor wife shall molest, annoy or in any way interfere with the other, or use any means to compel, or attempt to compel, the other to cohabit or live with him or her.

3. **CUSTODY:** The wife shall have sole custody, care and control of the children.

4. **ACCESS:**
   (1) The husband shall have access,
       (a) from ten in the morning until six o'clock in the evening of each Saturday; and
       (b) after the 14th to and including the 31st day of July in each year.
   (2) The husband shall exercise his right to access outside the children's home and shall make all necessary transportation arrangements to collect the children and return them later to their home.
   (3) Whenever the husband intends to exercise his right of access, he shall give notice of his intention to the wife,
       (a) on or before the preceding Wednesday for Saturday visits; and
       (b) on or before June 15 for the period mentioned in 1 (b).
   (4) If the husband fails to give notice under paragraph 4 (3) above, he shall not have access on the occasion for which notice was not given, but failure to give notice is not a waiver of his rights of access for later occasions.
   (5) The husband shall not have access where it might reasonably be detrimental to the children's health or well-being.
   (6) Neither husband nor wife may remove the children from the Province of Ontario without the consent in writing of the other.

5. **FINANCIAL SUPPORT:** On December 1, 1976, and on the first day of each month following, during the joint lives of the husband and wife, the husband shall pay to the wife,
   (a) the sum of $250 for her own support until she remarries or lives with a man as if she had remarried; and
   (b) $100 for each child for maintenance of that child (making a total of $200 for the children) until one or more of the following occurs,
       (i) the child becomes 16 years old and ceases to be in full-time attendance at an educational institution;
       (ii) the child ceases to reside with the wife;
       (iii) the child becomes 18 years old;
       (iv) the child marries; or
       (v) the child dies.

6. **MATERIAL CHANGE IN CIRCUMSTANCES:**
   (1) The husband and wife intend paragraphs 3, 4 and 5 of this agreement to be final except for variation by reason of a material change in circumstances.
   (2) Obligations arising out of the remarriage of the husband or

73  All about separation

of the wife or both are to be taken into account in determining whether there has been a material change in circumstances.

(3) If a material change in circumstances takes place, only the provisions in paragraphs 3, 4 and 5 of the Agreement may be varied.

(4) The husband or wife wanting the variation shall give to the other a notice of the variation he or she is seeking and the husband and wife may then confer with each other either personally or through their respective solicitors to settle what, if any, variation should be made.

(If no agreement on variation is reached within thirty clear days after notice has been given, the parties agree to arbitration by the appropriate provincial authority having jurisdiction over child welfare or the award of maintenance or alimony.)

7. **HEALTH AND MEDICAL EXPENSES:**
(The husband warrants that he is maintaining the available provincial health insurance plan to cover the wife and children and if he fails to make payments, all medical and hospital expenses will be his responsibility.)

8. **PERSONAL PROPERTY:** The husband and wife each acknowledge that:
   (a) all their personal property has been divided between them to their mutual satisfaction;
   (b) each is entitled to the personal property now in his or her possession free from any claim by the other; and
   (c) each may dispose of the personal property now possessed by him or her as if he or she were unmarried.

9. **MATRIMONIAL HOME:**
   (1) The husband and wife acknowledge that they hold as joint tenants the house and lot municipally known as 387 Pleasant Valley Drive . . ., and each agrees that the house and lot are to be sold and the net proceeds equally divided between them.
   (2) Upon division of the sale proceeds, all necessary accounts are to be taken and adjustments made so that from the date of separation until the date of sale, both husband and wife are to bear equally all charges relating to the house and lot including but not limited to mortgage payments, taxes, insurance premiums, expenses in maintaining the house and lot, and all expenses of sale.

10. **BAR OF DOWER:** The husband and wife acknowledge that simultaneously with the execution of this agreement the wife has executed a power of attorney appointing the husband her attorney for her and in her name to execute all deeds, transfers, mortgages, charges or other documents that are necessary to bar her dower or inchoate right to dower, whether legal or equitable, in any lands wherever located that the husband now owns or may afterwards acquire and to execute further or other powers of attorney for that purpose that the husband may reasonably require.

11. **DEBTS AND OBLIGATIONS:**
    (1) Neither the husband nor the wife shall contract in the name of the other nor in any way bind the other for any debts or obligations.
    (2) If debts or obligations are incurred by the husband or the wife on behalf of the other before or after the date of this agreement, he or she shall indemnify the other from all
       (a) claims;
       (b) costs;
       (c) expenses;
       (d) damages; and
       (e) actions,
       arising from those debts or obligations.

12. **SEPARATION AGREEMENT TO SURVIVE DIVORCE:** If either the husband or the wife obtains a decree of divorce, all the terms of this agreement shall survive and continue in force.

13. **INDEPENDENT LEGAL ADVICE:** The husband and wife each acknowledge that each,
    (a) has had independent legal advice;
    (b) understands their respective rights and obligations under this agreement; and
    (c) is signing this agreement voluntarily.

14. **WIFE'S LEGAL FEES AND DISBURSEMENTS:** The husband shall reimburse the wife for all legal fees and disbursements incurred by her in engaging the services of Freda Lam, Barrister and Solicitor, for the negotiation and preparation of this agreement.

IN WITNESS WHEREOF the husband and wife hereunto set their hands and seals.

SIGNED, SEALED AND DELIVERED

in the presence of

---

JANE LOUISE DOE

JOHN RICHARD DOE

A court may award damages for any failure to comply with the clauses in a separation agreement.

The sample agreement outlined here by no means exhausts all the possibilities of separation agreements. For instance, there is no mention of insurance policies carried by either spouse to establish which one will be responsible for paying the premiums and who will be the beneficiary, conditionally or forever.

There is also no reference to a release of claims and rights to any estate that one of the spouses might acquire during the separation, or a mention of one spouse acting as the administrator of the other's will or estate, or being excluded from same. It is a good precaution to agree to surrender to each other such documents as may be required in order to carry out the terms of the agreement. All of these are common accessories to separation agreements.

## Separated but under one roof

You don't have to be living apart in order to have a separation agreement or grounds for divorce under the marital breakdown clause. It is necessary, however, that there be evidence that sexual relations have stopped, that you are not performing domestic duties for your husband, and that the two of you have few common interests.

The law provides a rather touching allowance for one reconciliation attempt. It is not counted against you in a divorce action if you and your husband resume sexual relations for a period not to exceed ninety consecutive days. This cannot be broken up into overnight visits but must be concurrent and it can be counted as part of the separation period.

A British Columbia court decided in 1970 that a marriage had broken down sufficiently to qualify for a divorce even though the parties were living under the same roof. There was evidence that there had been no sexual or domestic relationship between them for three years.

Another divorce was refused even though the wife was ill and there had been no sexual or domestic relations on her part. She had invited her mother to live with them, however, and the mother did the housework, which the court decided was the equivalent of the wife performing those tasks herself and thereby maintaining her marriage.

Another woman who stayed in the home also occupied by her husband and did some housework herself was granted a divorce because she did nothing but what was necessary for her own needs and those of her children.

## Under two roofs but not separated

You are not necessarily separated, as the law construes separation, just because you are living apart with no sexual or domestic relationship, as when couples are parted by travel or hospitalization or imprisonment. So long as there is communication by mail, telephone, or visits, you're married.

One man whose wife was in a mental hospital for three years was refused a divorce on the grounds of separation because the court felt that physical separation wasn't the whole definition of "living separate and apart". A man who stopped visiting his wife in a mental hospital for five years, however, was judged to be separated from her.

# 7 All about desertion

If you walk out of your marriage, you may forfeit your flimsy dower right to the home and your right to have financial support from your husband. If you leave the children behind, it may jeopardize your right to have custody. And you will not be able to obtain a divorce after a three-year separation; if you are the one suing for divorce, you must wait for five years.

There is something called in law "constructive desertion", which means that the reasons for your departure were so compelling that you have not really deserted at all. These are adultery on your husband's part and/or mistreatment of you within the legal definition of cruelty. In those two situations you may leave without a loss of rights.

If you have any sexual relations after you leave your husband, even if your departure was necessary to save your life, you may forfeit everything. You cannot seek comfort in another man's bed without losing your right to a share in the home and the contents, as well as regular support payments, use of his credit, and so on. Husbands obtain title to their wives' sexual apparatus and this doesn't stop even if they are brutes.

The loss of rights that follows your fall from faithfulness is not necessarily final. If your husband forgives the adultery, takes you back into his home and resumes sexual relations with you for a period of more than ninety consecutive days, the law calls this "condoning" and your offense cannot count against you again.

Providing you are celibate, however, your husband or common-law husband must provide for you if he deserts you. The Criminal Code demands that men who abandon their mates must continue to pay for the necessities of life for them, and this obligation doesn't cease even if someone else, a friend or relative, is also helping the deserted woman. Men who fail to make provision for the women they leave are liable to arrest.

A common-law marriage is defined as one that appears to be a marriage—that is, the couple live at the same address, have sexual relations, are seen as a marriage by the neighbours, and share the chores, income, children, and whatever.

When there are children, financial responsibility for them is not influenced by desertion, adultery, or cruelty. It stays with the parents until the child reaches sixteen. A badly behaved parent may lose custody or even the right to see the children, but the financial obligation remains the same, and this applies to adopted or illegitimate children as well.

If your husband deserts, you are entitled to receive from him sufficient money to cover food, clothing, medical and legal expenses and the rent. This is contingent, it must be emphasized, on your chastity.

Failure to receive support from him is grounds for legal action. You handle your complaint either in a civil action by way of a writ or in the Family Court, where you file a summons.

You have just encountered the chaos of Canadian laws concerning the family. At present as many as five different courts may handle family problems and few of them have the necessary support services of psychiatry, psychology, counselling or adequate enforcement. The Law Reform Commission of Canada observed in its *Working Paper 1* on *The Family Court* that the higher the court, the less likely it is that it can take a flexible, co-operative approach to the tangle of family matters.

"It is significant," said the Law Reform Commission, "that the superior courts rarely invoke the assistance of agencies in the community to attempt to reconcile the parties or to promote conciliation or amicable settlements." It recommended, as provincial law reform commissions also do, that the provinces and federal governments unify family courts.

In the meantime, deserted women have two courts to choose from if they are destitute. The difference between using the higher court and the Family Court is one of social class: women who are poor are too desperate to wait for the leisurely aristocratic upper court so they must hurry to the quicker Family Court.

In return for speed, the Family Court imposes a ceiling on the financial support it will demand from the husband, so the poor woman or any woman whose situation is urgent will be allotted a small amount. The civil court has no ceiling and can assess the husband any amount that is reasonable to his circumstances. These courts often are clogged, and women who use them must be able to afford a long wait which is sometimes a year or more.

Women who apply for welfare assistance can receive it only if they go to the Family Court and obtain a support order against their husbands. This has been justified all these years by guardians of the public purse who point out that it is the man's responsibility, not the state's, and the man should be made to pay.

In fact, though, it results in almost no improvement in welfare costs. Very few men in low income categories are able or willing to pay support allowances. There is some evidence that the machinery to hunt and jail them is more costly to society than the welfare payment it is intended to save. In addition the compulsory court action increases bitterness between spouses and weakens the possibility of reconciliation.

The legal procedure is somewhat similar in both Family Court and the civil court. The judge hears the wife's story and decides whether or not the husband will be summonsed to appear. If the writ is issued and served, the husband must come to court eventually to defend his wife's action.

The hearing takes place in the form of a trial to bring forth evidence that the husband has deserted and is not providing for his family. If this is the situation, and the wife has no other inferred means of income, by which the law explicitly means a male friend, the court will examine the husband's resources and assess a proportion of them for the deserted family.

If the husband fails to make the payments, and many do, the process of trying to collect is dreary and degrading and usually fruitless. The wife must apply for another summons to be issued to him, and both must appear in court which will then inquire into the husband's reasons for failing to make the payments. If he is able to pay, he is ordered to do so. If not, the court will ask what efforts he is making to find employment and will attempt to press him to take what he can at once.

Canada's National Health and Welfare Minister Marc Lalonde said in May 1975, that some seventy-five per cent of all court orders for maintenance are defaulted. He pointed out that in some countries, such as Israel, the state is responsible for the collection and payment of allowances so women there are assured of support. The National Law Reform Commission has indicated that Canada should move in this direction as well.

Some women have gone to family court as many as a dozen times in their efforts to collect money that the court declared they should have. If the husband fails to turn up, as often happens, or otherwise exhausts the court's patience, he can be sent to jail. During this time, of course, it is impossible for the family to receive anything from him.

The National Law Reform Commission, in *Working Paper 1*,

recommends that provinces establish unified family courts to deal with all non-crime problems that families face; one court for divorces, change of name, alimony and maintenance, custody, adoptions, child neglect, separation orders, and the like. The paper makes a note of the laxity of enforcement of separation allowances: "It has been estimated that no less than 80,000 families in Canada are not being maintained by the responsible spouse or parent."

The courts are almost helpless when the spouse is mobile or jobless, but can garnishee wages and seize bank accounts when such exist in order to collect separation payments.

Most deserted wives with children have no choice but to apply for welfare or other public assistance. Most are only qualified for low-wage jobs, which will not cover the high cost of good day care, if day care even exists. They cannot upgrade their skills in job-training courses because they can't afford to have their children properly cared for in their absence.

And while all this distress is on her back, she must not have a male friend around. If she does she will lose her welfare payments or maintenance from her husband will cease.

## Legally dead

If your husband disappears, you can have him declared legally dead after seven years have passed without any word of his whereabouts. It will be necessary to show that serious attempts have been made to locate him but without success.

A presumption of death by the courts does not make you divorced or a widow. If you remarry you run the risk of your first husband turning up again, which will make the second marriage void.

Children of the second marriage, however, are regarded as legitimate.

# 8  All about divorce

The Divorce Act of 1968 swept away many of the obstacles to divorce that have existed since marriage was regarded as a God-welded bond that made the family an immutable unit. That kind of rigidity made for a solid, safe society and many see marriage break-up as a fundamental cause of today's uneasiness. The steady state, however, imprisoned some men and women for life with the impulsive choices of their youth. Marriage increasingly is being seen as a union that two people try in good faith but sever if it becomes full of pain.

During the century that Canada's divorce laws reflected Britain's 1857 Divorce and Matrimonial Causes Act, almost the only acceptable grounds for divorce was adultery. Until 1968, marriages broke up for the same complex reasons that they do today, but it was necessary every time to prove a single fault: adultery. To accommodate the law it was normal for husbands to arrange scenes of adultery with paid women, called co-respondents, usually supplied by the detective who agreed to surprise the illicit couple and testify to their amorous disarray.

This band of thespians went out of business in 1968 when the laws were broadened to recognize that adultery may be a symptom of marriage breakdown but it is rarely a cause.

Adultery, however, remains crucial to divorce settlements. Intercourse with a third person influences alimony, maintenance, and even the custody of children.

The law defines adultery as voluntary sexual intercourse by any married person with another person not his or her spouse. Both parties must be willing and both must have the mental capacity to understand what they are doing. It isn't adultery if a spouse copulates while drunk, psychotic or drugged; it isn't adultery if the wife is raped.

Sexual relations before the wedding are not considered as adultery and cannot be grounds for divorce, even if the woman is pregnant by someone not her husband.

Artificial insemination presents some intriguing legal problems. In 1921 (Orford v. Orford) a judge ruled that a wife committed adultery when she attempted to become pregnant by means of donor semen without her husband's consent. It reflects the law's view that a wife's reproductive organs belong to the husband and cannot be exercised or removed without his consent.

No divorce has ever been sought in Canada for artificial insemination without the husband's permission. Doctors who enable women to become pregnant by this means take care to ensure that the husband is aware and agreeable.

The spouse who makes the charge of adultery has the responsibility of proving it. If you are suing your husband for divorce on the grounds of adultery, he doesn't have to prove he is innocent—you have to prove he's guilty. It is an important difference.

Canadian courts are not enthusiastic about evidence of adultery presented by private detectives: it revives in judges' minds the memory of those cornball motel setups of the 1950s. Judges register their displeasure by being critical of the detective's breezy methods. One divorce was refused because the witness to adultery, a paid detective, entered the bedroom illegally, coming in through the window.

The courts generally prefer testimony from neutral sources such as the police or motel operator. Judges don't need eyewitness accounts of coitus. If the couple spent the night in a motel or hotel room, and the desk clerk testifies to this, the court will infer that a sexual act took place.

## Bars to a divorce

It is possible to have a perfect divorce action, with clear proof that legal grounds exist, and still have it thrown out of court. If there has been collusion between you and your husband in your anxiety to obtain a trouble-free judgment, the slightest evidence of it will cause the judge to throw you both out on your ears.

Collusion means that you have agreed to stage adultery, or agreed to institute court proceedings, or agreed beforehand not to claim damages or ask for a settlement. The law doesn't prevent you and your husband from meeting to discuss reconciliation, or from discussing ancillary matters that precede divorce. But you must not manipulate the court by deciding what he'll say and what you'll say in order to get the verdict that suits you. You are being divorced: the court wants you to act in an irreconcilable manner.

It is not uncommon to make a pre-divorce agreement about who will pay the court costs. Chivalry used to compel men to be the guilty party. They would ask their wives to sue them, in appreciation of which they would assume the legal expenses. It amounts to a purchase of divorce and is borderline collusion, but probably would not result in the divorce being refused if the judge happened to know about it.

There are two circumstances which can bar a divorce at the judge's discretion, which means they aren't necessarily a bar, as collusion is. One is connivance and the other condonation.

Connivance is really any corrupt act by either spouse to promote or encourage the other into an adulterous affair, or a show of indifference that the affair is happening. It is active connivance, for instance, if your husband arranges matters in such a way as to set you up for adultery. If he leases a remote summer cottage, invites your old love for the weekend and then disappears, that's active connivance, to say the least.

Also, if he suspects that you are having an affair on Wednesdays and he fakes a Wednesday out-of-town trip in order to catch you in the act, that's connivance.

Another possible bar to divorce is condonation. It means "forgiveness of a conjugal offense with the full knowledge of all the circumstances." Once forgiveness for adultery or cruelty or desertion has been demonstrated by a reunion of the couple that extends more than ninety consecutive days, the judge may refuse to grant a divorce. You can insist that the attempt to repair the marriage turned out disastrously on the ninety-first day, but the judge can still rule that it has a mendable look.

In one interesting decision a husband wrote to his wife expressing the wish that "bygones be bygones." The court decided that the phrase was sufficiently general to cover all the offenses that the husband knew about when he wrote it, as well as the ones he learned about subsequently. His petition for divorce was refused.

Condonation is forgiveness of what has already transpired. It does not encompass future activities. If there is a later breach of a similar or different nature that is covered in the Divorce Act, proceedings can be instituted.

There's a kind of condonation born of passivity. You must not, as lawyers put it, "go to sleep on your rights". If you tolerate adultery or cruelty for a long time, you are assumed to like it that way. The court will not hasten to your side to help you out of the marriage, unless you can demonstrate that the delay was the result of the absence of legal advice, or ignorance of your rights, or hope for improvement in the situation, or concern for children.

84   The Law is not for Women

Under present legislation, lawyers are required to inform their clients that marriage counselling is available. This statute was intended to encourage couples to make an effort to resolve their differences by means of professional help. It is not obligatory to see a counsellor.

## Grounds for divorce: cruelty

Since Bill C-187 was enacted on July 2, 1968, there is a range of grounds for divorce that cover almost every situation except the most common one, that people don't want to be married to one another any longer.

The traditional grounds of adultery are still the most commonly used; it is a relatively simple, no-fuss situation to prove. Cruelty, on the other hand, is complex.

Before 1968, Nova Scotia was the only province that permitted divorce on the grounds of cruelty, by which it meant a physical battering once or many times of shocking severity. In other provinces a woman could not be divorced from a husband who beat her.

The present legislation embraces both physical and mental cruelty, which are such vague terms that such divorce actions are dependent upon the human sensibilities of the judge rather than the usual body of precedents and regulations.

Unlike the practice in some jurisdictions in the United States, cruelty in Canada means what it says and doesn't extend to the irritation of cracker crumbs in bed or belching. It must be shown without question that it was impossible for reasons of safety for the victimized spouse to remain in the marriage.

For instance, if you are planning to divorce your husband for cruelty, you must have proof that your husband's conduct was dangerous to a degree to destroy your health or sanity, or that you have reason to fear that his conduct would wreck you if you lived with it any longer. It isn't necessary that he actually hit you; severe emotional stress amounts to abuse as well.

You must be in a state of fear before any court will call your husband's behaviour cruelty. Mere apprehension is not considered adequate grounds for divorce, even if you have been bruised or harassed.

Saskatchewan and Alberta courts are inclined to restrict the definition of cruelty to conduct which is dangerous to life, limb, or health, or is "so grossly insulting as to be intolerable". Quebec courts recognize the more subtle forms of interpersonal destruction and appreciate such flavours as outrage, ill-usage or grievous insult. In 1969 an

Ontario judge described cruelty as behaviour "of such a kind as to render intolerable the continued cohabitation of the spouses"—but what one judge can tolerate may not be the same as another judge's views on mayhem.

Cruelty need not be intentional. Conduct founded on delusions of such a kind that the person is not exactly insane can be the basis of a divorce such as when a person's delusional behaviour makes existence unpleasant for the spouse.

There have been some curious examples of cruelty accepted by Canadian courts. One woman was divorced on the grounds of cruelty because her husband was a transvestite, another because her husband had sexual relations with children. In British Columbia in 1970, a woman wanted a divorce because her husband had become a hippie and smoked marijuana. She called it cruelty but the court decided it wasn't; her divorce was granted on the grounds of marriage breakdown instead.

In 1970, in British Columbia, the judge called it cruelty when a husband was shown to have ignored his wife except to make unreasonable sexual demands and to have neglected her medical needs.

There was an interesting precedent in a divorce granted in Ontario in 1974 on the grounds of cruelty. County Court Judge H.S. Honsberger decided that the young wife of a heroin addict had suffered from mental cruelty during the five months she knew of his addiction. Most judges have not accepted this route around the provision in the Divorce Act that the spouse of someone grossly addicted to alcohol or drugs can obtain a divorce upon proof that the addiction had extended over a minimum of three years, but Judge Honsberger ruled that this was an exceptional situation.

Courts are sensitive to the feelings of people who suffer a barrage of ridicule. A man in Nova Scotia whose wife continually belittled him, reducing his efficiency at work, was granted a divorce; so was one in British Columbia whose wife sneered at his sexual performance, comparing him unfavourably with a previous husband and some lovers. The judge observed sympathetically, "There is little doubt in my mind that if he had not left he would have become a prime candidate for the mental hospital."

A Saskatchewan woman was given a divorce because it was shown that her husband's critical, intolerant and overbearing attitude caused her to become severely depressed. A woman in Nova Scotia who was described as sensitive was given a divorce from a domineering husband; so was an Ontario woman, whose husband berated her continually.

Another woman in Nova Scotia obtained a divorce because her husband was an excessive drinker, refused to help with the housework or discipline the children, and insisted that she hold a full-time job. Her case was assisted by medical evidence that she had developed ulcers which required surgery. In the same province a woman was divorced from a man with a violent temper, who threw furniture and threatened to hit her, sometimes injuring himself in his rage. A New Brunswick woman was divorced from a wife-beater, a heavy drinker who used to lock her out of the house.

A man in British Columbia complained that his wife was "unreasonably independent and lacked submissiveness", and obtained a divorce. An Ontario woman was divorced because her husband forced her to perform the oral-genital act of fellatio against her will. New Brunswick courts also decided that "abnormal sexual activities" imposed by one spouse on another were sufficient grounds for divorce.

Divorces have been refused in cases where one spouse complained of sexual incompatibility (she said her husband was lacking in affection), where the husband rarely spoke to his wife, where the husband could not hold a job, where the couple argued about religion, where the husband was a terminal case of hypochondria, where the husband liked to masturbate while looking at girlie magazines, where the woman was obsessively fastidious, where the wife nagged about her husband's neglect of her for civic affairs.

The court often rules against divorce petitions on the grounds of cruelty if there is evidence that the alleged victim wasn't greatly concerned by whatever was going on. A wife who wanted to divorce her husband because he was often away all night was refused because she couldn't show that her mental health was in jeopardy. Another woman who was mistreated for years by a drunk and abusive man was not given a divorce because she had put up with it for such a long time.

Similarly, a man who wanted a divorce because his wife refused to have sex with him was refused. The marriage had been consummated and the judge ruled that the man wasn't suffering unduly by her decision.

## Marriage breakdown

Marriage breakdown is a catch-all category. It includes gross addiction to alcohol or narcotics for a period of not less than three years, a provision some judges evade by calling a shorter time of addiction mental cruelty.

Separation is marriage breakdown after three years of living apart, with no more than ninety days of trial reconciliation permitted in the interval, the ninety days to be consecutive and not several random tries. If the person seeking the divorce deserted the spouse, the separation must be for five years.

When a couple has been separated for three years out a five-year period because one of them is in jail, the other can sue for divorce. If a spouse is given a sentence of ten years or more, and all attempts to reduce the sentence by appeal have failed, the other can be granted a divorce after two years.

If a spouse has disappeared for three years and cannot be located after serious attempts to do so have been made, the deserted spouse can apply for a divorce.

There is also provision for non-consummation of the marriage for the year following the ceremony, which is a less-encumbered alternative to annulment. It must be shown that the person seeking the divorce has been unable by reason of illness or disability or unwillingness to consummate the marriage.

In Ontario there was a case of a wife who lived with her husband for two months after the ceremony, refusing to consummate their relationship, and then disappeared. He was granted a divorce.

A divorce in British Columbia was refused even though there was evidence of non-consummation. In that case the marriage had been contracted in order to facilitate immigration and the parties had never lived together. The judge ruled that there was no refusal to consummate and dismissed the application.

A Manitoba court ruled in 1973 that the fact a couple admitted to sexual relations before marriage did not have any bearing on the subsequent refusal by one of them to consummate the marriage after the ceremony. Divorce was granted. That same year a Manitoba man whose marriage of eleven years had never been consummated was also granted a divorce. The court ruled, however, that some form of marriage did exist over that long period.

## Sodomy, bestiality and rape

These are defined in the Divorce Act as grounds for a decree. Sodomy (or buggery) is sexual intercourse involving the penis of one person and the anus of another, male or female. Bestiality is sexual intercourse between a person and an animal; it is also a criminal offence. A husband who has been convicted of rape can be sued for divorce. In two cases, one in Ontario in 1970 and one in Manitoba in 1974, divorce was granted even though the man had not be convicted of the charge.

It is not possible for a wife to obtain a divorce if her husband rapes her unless she does so on the grounds of cruelty.

## Homosexuality

If one partner in a marriage is homosexual and this can be proved or admitted, it is grounds for divorce.

Some courts react excitedly to even a suggestion of homosexuality. A Saskatoon judge granted a man a divorce because his wife caressed the breasts of another woman, and in Prince Edward Island in 1972 a man was able to divorce his wife because she had an orgasm while fondling a woman.

## Matrimonial property

That's whatever property he owns, or you own, or you both own. In Quebec progressive legislation may ensure that everything either of you purchased after the marriage, or in some cases before your marriage, is jointly owned no matter who paid for it. In the other provinces there is strong pressure from such groups as Status of Women Action Committees, generally with the support of the local Law Reform Commission, to bring the law concerning matrimonial property in line with Quebec's.

Quebec excludes from joint ownership what is designated as *private property*, by which it means, usually, property owned by each before the wedding, or property inherited by one or the other, or benefits from an insurance policy or pension plan, or such personal things as clothing, decorations, diplomas and correspondence.

Everything else is mutually owned, fifty-fifty. You and your husband share equally in the total financial product of the marriage. For the first time in Canada it is being recognized that the unpaid contribution of a wife is as valuable to the marriage as the income provided by the husband.

At the time of writing, Ontario was considering revisions in its matrimonial property legislation. These changes would not affect separate ownership of property during the existence of the marriage, (which is the traditional split that keeps most women paupers and makes it impossible for them to obtain credit in their own names,) but would offer deferred community ownership. This would mean that sharing of the property would begin if the marriage breaks up. It was suggested also that it cover only one home. If one partner owns more than one home, the courts would decide whether the woman's claim should extend to the others.

In the Northwest Territories, where few people own their homes, legislation now protects women by empowering judges to evaluate the work of each partner when distributing the assets of a marriage —that's both paid and unpaid work.

Saskatchewan, with a province full of farm wives increasingly concerned about their rights after the Murdoch decision, has a government slow to move to community ownership legislation. There is much opinion that joint ownership would be too "rigid, inconvenient and inefficient". Alberta also was looking at a modest plan, leaving the sharing to the decision of judges rather than imposing it. The Alberta Institute of Law Research and Reform has recommended, however, that during a marriage one partner should not be permitted to squander the assets that might later be properly claimed by the other.

British Columbia's Royal Commission on Family and Children's Law, better known as the Berger Commission, has the most advanced proposals. It believes that deferring community rights until such time as there is a divorce works a hardship on wives. It notes that in the past whenever there is flexibility in the exercise of ownership, women suffer. It therefore recommends not only joint ownership of property acquired after marriage but joint management of that property. Neither spouse could make deals without the consent of the other.

If the provinces and territories come out with a variety of matrimonial property laws, a couple which moves about and buys land in more than one province is obviously going to give the courts a big pain if there is a divorce. The federal government can legislate grounds for divorce, but there is the BNA Act in the way of making the Divorce Act cover matrimonial property. The Law Reform Commission of Canada is looking for solutions to make the provinces somewhat uniform in this regard, but there isn't much optimism on the subject.

What may happen is a law which states that the first domicile is the operative one and that provincial laws where it is situated will apply to property out of the province, or that the law may declare that "habitual residence" will determine which province has jurisdiction over the settlement.

In the meantime, except in Quebec and the Northwest Territories you have no clear right to anything you haven't paid for yourself. If you had no independent income which you put into the house and its content, you have no vested right even to a teabag.

It does not follow that if you can prove you put money into the property, you necessarily have at least partial ownership, as Irene Murdoch discovered in Alberta. For instance, Lida Madisso of Peterborough, Ontario, was married for thirty years and had a full-time job most of those years, during which she helped her husband buy a house and a cottage. He deserted her, fathered a child with another woman, and refused to pay her alimony. When she was divorced in April 1975, Mr. Justice Meyer Lerner ruled that her husband obviously had no intention of sharing the house or cottage ownership with her. In that case, he said, she had no legal basis for her half-interest claim even though the cottage was at one time in her name alone. He assessed the husband $150 a month maintenance, and that was all she got for thirty years of contributing to the marriage.

Mr. Justice David McDonald of the Alberta Supreme Court suggested some precautions wives might take:

- When the assets are purchased, you should have a conversation in front of witnesses in which your husband says clearly, "Half of it belongs to you, dear," or, preferably, "Half of everything I have is yours, dear."
- You should keep a record of the number of times you entertain your husband's clients or employers and their wives.
- You should pay part of the purchase price of the house and have proof that you did.
- You should keep a record of the times you shovel the walk or put on the storm windows, or any other task traditionally held to be the man's responsibility.
- You should keep a record of the times your husband asks or orders you not to take a job because he wants you in the home.

It seems likely that reform in matrimonial property laws is imminent in those parts of the country still without them, and such belligerent record-keeping will not be needed. It has been slow in coming because it has some tricky aspects that would work as inequitably as the old laws. For instance, some are concerned that when matrimonial property is divided in two, the industrious spouse is penalized and the lazy one rewarded.

There is also doubt about the consequences of the reform on marriage choices. A man who has been married once to a woman who didn't contribute financially must give up half his assets to her, assets perhaps acquired in his peak achievement years, and comes impoverished into a second marriage and further depleted if there is a third. The most desirable males, from a mercenary point of view, therefore, will be those who have not been pruned by having been married before, and the most desirable women will be those enriched by at least one previous marriage.

Men and women with high qualifications for big-income jobs might postpone marriage until they have acquired a stockpile of assets, since the property they own before the wedding can't be touched upon divorce.

There is little evidence, however, that people are so cold-blooded when they marry.

The larger concern surrounding matrimonial property reform is whether or not it should be accompanied by abandonment of alimony and maintenance payments, since the women will emerge from a marriage with assets equal to those of the man. The Law Reform Commission of Canada's *Working Paper 12*, largely the work of Edward F. Ryan, noted that women remain in a disadvantaged position after a marriage if they have not been keeping up their career developments as the man has.

It proposed "catch-up" maintenance payments to a spouse who has remained at home during the marriage by mutual choice and that other than this, temporary funding maintenance should be provided only when the spouse is incapacitated physically or mentally or unable to work for other reasons. Children's maintenance would be the responsibility of both parents, the proportions to be fixed according to incomes.

In *Working Paper 8*, the Law Reform Commission reviewed Family Property and noted that many couples do not have substantial assets to divide, particularly as private home ownership continues to decline in Canada. In those situations elimination of maintenance would leave the spouse who has been out of the work force at a severe disadvantage. It recommends, therefore, that "The property position of a spouse seeking maintenance in divorce proceedings will simply be another factor to be considered by the court in deciding whether a maintenance award would be appropriate, and if so, how much and for how long."

A parallel societal change will have to be women's incomes and opportunities. The whole system of alimony and maintenance was instituted because it was seen that women were unable to support themselves nearly so well as men could. This inequity still exists.

## Joint bank account

This is an uncertain area, full of injustice. If you had no income of your own during the marriage, the court may divide the bank balance in half. If must be demonstrated that it was your husband's intent when the account was established that you two should share it. If you deposited all the money from your earnings, the court will give the total amount to you—your husband does not get half.

If you both have been earning and contributing to the bank account, it probably will be divided equally, though some courts take into consideration disparity in incomes and cut the pie to match.


## Who is at fault?

Divorce courts are still preoccupied under the terms of the Divorce Act with identifying who is to blame for a marriage failure. There is, even in the category of Marriage Breakdown, a stacking of the evidence to determine which partner is a villain and which a saint, all of which is palpable nonsense. It is a pageant with a real victim, however, when the court comes to the moment of awarding maintenance. The so-called guilty party is likely to get hurt.

The current trend, however, is toward court neutrality in judgments concerning money. It is a recognition that guilt and innocence are unfathomable in a human relationship, and irrelevant in a divorce action.

There was an interesting decision in New Zealand in 1973 in the case of *Wachtel v. Wachtel*. The Court of Appeal held that even though conduct of each partner is to be considered, there should be no "post mortem to find out what killed the marriage" and no "discount" or "reduction" in the settlement because the wife was partly to blame.

Since January 1976, Australian couples are now able to obtain a divorce after twelve months' separation, no questions asked.


## Quickie divorces elsewhere

These are more rare than they used to be before Canada's liberalized divorce legislation, but it is still not uncommon for couples in a hurry to have one partner establish residence for a few weeks in some other country and file petition for a divorce there. It is highly likely that the divorce will not conform to Canadian law and will therefore be invalid. It is possible that subsequent marriages by either spouse could be declared bigamous by the courts, though no such action has ever been laid.

## Do-it-yourself divorce

Law societies have moved ponderously to shut off the threat to income, which was real, and the possibility of self-administered injustice, which was less real, when do-it-yourself divorce kits were available, chiefly in British Columbia and Ontario.

It is still possible to weave your way yourself through the maze of affidavits and petitions that must be completed to obtain a simple, uncontested, no-property-or-children-involved, divorce. Your local Status of Women Action Committee may be able to help you, or the Women's Caucus of a law school, or the Women's Centre in your community.

If you are broke and there is legal aid available, apply there. Otherwise the rate for a lawyer may start at $500 for a simple divorce action and can cost $10,000 or more.

## Alimony and maintenance

The terms are interchangeable only to lay people. In law, alimony is the allowance granted when married people are separated; maintenance is the allowance paid after divorce to the financially disabled partner. Almost invariably the money flow goes from the husband or ex-husband to the wife or ex-wife.

The courts grant support to the woman under three conditions when there is separation: the husband had deserted, the husband has committed adultery; the husband has been cruel more often and more viciously than the court can bear—tolerance varies. The usual award to a woman who has no other income is one-third of the husband's net income after taxes. The amount is at the discretion of the court, however, and can be adjusted to fit individual circumstances. If both you and your husband are employed, the court may add the incomes together and equalize them. Since women almost invariably earn less than men, this results in a payment from the man to the woman but it is not inconceivable that it would go the other way in a case of an executive wife and low-income husband who had custody of children.

The person receiving the alimony and child support allowance pays income tax on it. The person paying is permitted to deduct the amount from total earnings and pays tax on the remainder.

Capital assets also are taken into consideration. Some time ago a court ruled that a wife should receive half her husband's income of a meager $5,200 a year; the husband also owned his home, a car, and property worth about $150,000 a year. Courts generally are guided by the practice of Ecclesiastical Courts which ruled on divorce actions prior to 1857. These courts used to award the wife one-fifth to one-third of the husband's income but, as a Canadian judge who exceeded that ratio recently commented, the Ecclesiastical Court "not only ascertained what moneys the husband had, but what moneys he could have had if he liked."

Alimony ceases if you are not celibate. The law never envisioned that a woman could have a sex drive or lovers who wouldn't be paying her.

Maintenance is slightly different. It is the allowance established by the court as part of the divorce action. In our sterner past, a woman divorced by her husband because she had committed adultery was viewed as such a fallen creature that the husband didn't have to give her a penny of settlement. The courts no longer refuse to grant maintenance when the woman has been proven adulterous.

Husbands can sue their wives for maintenance or alimony during the divorce proceedings where the economic conditions warrant it, and recent reforms in the law put the obligation to provide for children on both parents, rather than the father alone.

In April 1970, Mr. Justice Osler of the Supreme Court of Ontario heard the case of a man sued for divorce by his wife, from whom he had been separated for seventeen years, after giving to her property that had accumulated in value to about $150,000. It was earning her an annual income of some $10,000, while he was destitute and living on welfare. The court ruled that she should pay her husband maintenance of $335 a month.

The court can award interim alimony upon receiving a petition for divorce, before the divorce action is actually heard. If the woman is employed at a reasonable salary, such alimony is not likely to be granted. Even if the couple and assorted attorneys have agreed on a certain financial arrangement, the court has the authority to throw it out and decree another one.

# Sample petition for divorce

IN THE SUPREME COURT OF ONTARIO

BETWEEN

JANE LOUISE DOE

PETITIONER

and

JOHN RICHARD DOE and
ELIZABETH HARPER

PETITION FOR DIVORCE

*To This Honourable Court*
I hereby petition for a decree of divorce from the Respondent spouse, John Richard Doe, and for an order for interim custody of the children of the marriage, custody of the said children, interim alimony and disbursements, permanent maintenance for myself and the said children, or in the alternative alimony and child-maintenance and costs on the grounds and in the circumstances following:

1. Grounds:

A.  My Petition is under the DIVORCE ACT (CANADA) section 3, subsection (a).

B.  The particulars of my grounds for divorce are:
    1.  On or about the 6th day of July, 1975, at the Royal Hotel at 922 Main Street in the City of Belleville in the Province of Ontario the Respondent spouse committed adultery with his co-respondent.
    2.  With full knowledge of his adultery, I resumed cohabitation with the Respondent spouse on or about the 14th day of July, 1975, for the purpose of reconciliation and continued cohabitation for that purpose until on or about the 17th day of August, 1975, but a reconciliation was not effected.
    3.  From on or about the 17th day of August, 1975, to the date of this petition, the Respondent spouse has cohabited with his co-respondent and while so cohabiting frequently committed adultery with her.

2. Reconciliation:

A.  The particulars of the circumstances which may assist the Court in ascertaining whether there is a possibility of reconciliation or resumption of cohabitation are:
    1.  The particulars described in paragraph 1(b) above.
    2.  My solicitor has discussed with me the possibility of a reconciliation with the said respondent and has informed me of some of the marriage counselling and guidance facilities available in my community. My solicitor has also drawn my

attention to the provisions of the law which have as their object the effecting where possible of a reconciliation.

3. I no longer feel any affection for the respondent.
4. I do not wish to resume cohabitation with the respondent.

B: The following efforts to reconcile have been made:
1. I resumed cohabitation with the Respondent for the purpose of reconciliation in the circumstances described in paragraph 1(b).
2. During this period of cohabitation the Respondent and I received counselling on our differences from the Blue Feather Family Services in the Municipality of Ottawa, involving a total of four private interviews and six sessions of group therapy.

(Then follows Particulars of Marriage, which encompasses birth places of the spouses and where the wedding took place, Domicile and Jurisdiction, Age and Disability which establishes that each spouse is over 18 and sound of mind, and, under CHILDREN, the names and dates of birth of the children.)

B. The particulars of the past, present and proposed custody, care, upbringing and education of the said child(ren) are as follows:
1. At all times since the respondent spouse and I began to live separate and apart, the children have remained with me under my care and control at 387 Pleasant Valley Drive.
2. Our home at the said address is a three bedroom house which has adequate space and facilities to meet the needs and requirements of the children.
3. Richard attends Tee Bird Public School and Carolyn attends Children's Centre Day Care in our neighbourhood where they are making satisfactory progress.
4. I am employed three afternoons a week at Children's Centre Day Care and I am therefore able to devote almost full time to caring for the children.
5. I propose that custody of the said children be given to me and that they continue to reside with me under my care and control.
6. I propose that the children continue their formal education to the extent that their abilities allow.

(If the father is protesting application for custody, his claim is noted next).

### 8. Separation Agreements and Financial Arrangements

(Both spouses list their financial holdings, their incomes and the value of such property as the house and automobile.)

### 9. Collusion, Condonation and Connivance

(It is stated that there has been none.)

### 10. Relief Asked:

I therefore ask this Honourable Court for the following relief:

A. A decree that I be divorced from the respondent, John Richard

Doe;
B.  Maintenance, or, in the alternative, alimony;
C.  Custody of the children of the marriage;
D.  Maintenance for the said children;
E.  Interim custody of the said children;
F.  Interim alimony in the amount of $150.00 weekly;
G.  Interim disbursements;
H.  Costs;
I.  Such further or other relief as this Honourable Court deems just.

## Domicile

You are divorced in the province in which the petitioner for the divorce lives at the time the petition is made. It used to be that wives were considered to be domiciled wherever the husband lived, but this has been changed. If you are suing for divorce and you live in Saskatchewan, you file your petition with the Saskatchewan court even if your husband has gone to Pago Pago.

If you move to Nova Scotia after filing your petition, you cannot transfer your divorce action to that province.

The court considers domicile to mean that you had an address within that province for at least a year before you filed the petition, and that you lived in that residence for at least ten months of the year.

In some cases it isn't necessary that you actually live in the residence the stipulated time. If your occupation requires you to travel, for instance, or if you are in the armed services, you can claim to be a resident in the province where you make your headquarters.

## Divorce Reform

It is likely that reforms in Canada's Divorce Act will simplify the present clutter and confusion of definitions and accusations so that people who agree that their marriage has broken down may be divorced quickly and inexpensively with a statement to that effect certified before a judge.

The new divorce laws in England permit as grounds the fact that "the marriage has broken down irretrievably ..." It does not permit such a divorce, however, until the couple has been married for at least three years.

Additional grounds in England since 1973, annulling a marriage, are the presence of communicable venereal disease at the time of the ceremony, or the discovery that the bride was pregnant by someone other than the groom.

A parliamentary committee in Sweden worked for three years drafting divorce reform for that country and recommended that marriages be dissolved instantly, rather than wait for a year of separation. The principle underlying the proposal is that marriage should be voluntary cohabitation and would no longer exist if either word became inoperative.

There have been a number of recommendations for changes in Canada's divorce laws. The Canadian Bar Association has a Family Law Section which proposed that all the complex nit-picky grounds for divorce that now exist should be abandoned, clearing the way for people who want a divorce for any reason to have it after they have lived apart for a year. Divorce decrees would be held up only when there was a dispute over maintenance or custody of children.

This simple divorce has the feature that many other reform groups have suggested: the so-called "no fault" hearing. At present husband and wife bring evidence of neglect or mistreatment against one another in order to establish grounds for divorce and the court decides that one or the other is to blame for the marriage failure.

It forces unreality on an already painful situation, since it never happens in a human relationship breakdown that one person is wholly wrong and the other wholly right, and it also serves to exacerbate the ill will between the man and woman, a particularly deplorable outcome when children are involved.

"In our opinion," the Law Reform Commission of Canada stated in *Working Paper 13, Divorce,* "divorce procedures should be fundamentally revised. Instead of being primarily contentious, they should be more investigatory and directed to the best disposition or adjustment of the family situation as a whole."

It notes with some asperity that public interest has never demanded an investigation of two people who want to marry and it is baffling that courts and laws play such a heavy role in divorce.

"If the differences lead to constant friction and turmoil," the *Working Paper* adds, "the public interest can be promoted by separation and divorce."

The Law Reform Commission does not recommend a mandatory period of separation, giving instances of a woman who wanted a divorce from her husband because he had killed their children and another woman of fifty whose marriage had broken down irretrievably as examples of situations where a one-year wait would be unreasonable. It proposed instead a sort of divorce on demand but with provision for fence-mending reconciliation efforts if one spouse objects to the divorce.

The Chief Justice of Ontario's Family Courts, H.T.G. Andrews, is on record approving this arrangement. He also favours divorce on demand, providing the courts have some machinery to explore the marriage to determine if it is indeed beyond salvaging and to offer appropriate help.

The pressure to stiffen divorce laws rather than relax them comes from the element in society which sees divorce as part of a moral disintegration of values. They point out that easy divorce would lead to the impulsive destruction of marriages that might otherwise have weathered the thin time.

Divorce is slow and expensive in Canada but it is becoming increasingly common. In 1973 there were 36,704 divorces granted. Almost two-thirds were sought by women.

# 9 You work (for pay)

Except for those physically or mentally incapacitated, all women work. This chapter is restricted to those who are paid for what they do.

The proportion of women in the labour force was around thirteen per cent at the turn of the century. In 1974 it had risen to forty per cent and was still growing. A head count that year established the figure at 3,324,000 women wage-earners in the country. Substantial as that ratio is, Sweden, Japan, Britain, the United States, West Germany and Australia, in that order, have a higher percentage of women in their labour forces.

An analysis of Canadian working women was carried in *The Financial Post* in May 1975. Most working women, it appeared, are younger than thirty-five; most working women are married.

Lita-Rose Betcherman, former director of the women's bureau of the Ontario Department of Labour, once commented that in the future there will be "no more life-time careers in motherhood, no more full-time homemakers." Canada is fast approaching a time when all women will be raised with the expectation that they will hold a job, just as men are.

Wages, opportunities for promotion, and training programs still reflect society's attitude that women are not serious employees. Women quit to get married or have a baby, the reasoning goes, and therefore are not as valuable as men who, bound by head-of-household responsibilities, might stay with one firm until retirement.

It is simply not true. About forty-three per cent of women in the labour force work because they must: they are self-supporting. Married women usually work because the family needs two incomes: fifty per cent of working wives are married to men who earned less than $8,000 in 1974. Not infrequently, the married woman's income is the only one in the family because the husband is a student, or an invalid, or unemployed.

Yet women's incomes on the average are forty-five per cent lower than men's. As 1975—International Women's Year—drew to a close there was still not comprehensive federal human rights code covering women's employment and access to advancement; federal and provincial equal pay laws were not working, there were disparities in employee benefits available to a woman, and women promoted to a management level was still news.

The most common method for evading equal pay laws is for the employer to give the male employee a different title. Offices have executive assistants (men) and secretaries (women), or building maintenance operators (men) and cleaners (women).

When starting salaries for men and women are identical, men rapidly pull ahead because they are three times as likely to be selected for upward-mobility training programs. Management, when pressed to explain the total absence of women in the board room or at executive level, then explains sadly, "None of our ladies is qualified."

The series of articles in *The Financial Post* in the spring of 1975, intensively researched and lucidly written by James E. Bennett and Pierre Loewe, Toronto management consultants, reported that *"without exception* [italics theirs] women hold little decision-making power." Their survey of Canadian business and industry showed that women had reached management positions in a range of from one to ten per cent of the executives studied, even though women predominate in such industries as clothing manufacturing (seventy-six per cent are women), banking (seventy per cent), telephone communication (fifty-four per cent), and miscellaneous personal services industries (fifty-nine per cent).

Few women have complained and fewer still are successful. Joan McLellan, fired by the CTV network in 1972 after she charged her employer with sex discrimination, is an example. Her complaint was that she was one of four reporters on a national news show and all of them performed the same function. But she made between $2,000 and $3,000 a year less than the others, who were all men.

The case dragged through the courts and at every level her rich employer simply explained that she wasn't as competent as the men in that department. Judge after judge believed it and ruled against her. As International Women's Year ended, she was still appealing, though her legal costs had put her deeply in debt.

A woman in the police force in Sault Ste. Marie was paid less than her male counterparts and was passed over for promotion. When she took her complaint to the Supreme Court of Ontario in 1968, the judge ruled that lower pay was justified for women because it fit with "every rule of economics, civilization, family life, and common sense."

"Equal pay laws unhappily have not achieved equal pay for women workers as set out in the statutes," Sylva Gelber, director of the

Women's Bureau of the federal Department of Labour, commented in April 1974, at a Montreal meeting to which heads of business and industry had been invited to discuss women in the work force. Most of them didn't attend.

The disparity between the salaries of men and women has been increasing, in fact.

The mythology about women employees is that they aren't reliable, that they aren't really interested in their jobs and therefore are bad risks in training programs, and that they aren't in any case as capable as men.

On the contrary, women in the labour force are, on the average, younger than men, better educated, and the difference in absenteeism is negligible (0.5 per cent in Public Service) or non-existent. As for willingness to accept promotion, two-thirds of men answer that in the affirmative and one-half of women, a difference that may reflect a realistic scaling-down of ambition.

Banks are outstanding examples of discrimination against women. They are in the midst of hasty attempts to improve the situation, but in 1975 only 1.2 per cent of branch managers were women. Statistics Canada in 1971 reported that sixty-six per cent of women who worked in banks then earned less than $2.50 an hour, while only 10.6 per cent of men in banks earned less than $2.50 an hour.

The comprehensive Financial Post series reported that a woman is about twenty times less likely to earn more than $20,000 a year than is a man, and three to four times more likely to earn less than $6,000.

The federal government has taken leadership in legislating against discrimination directed at working women but the government is a major offender. Of all the women in the federal public service, eighty-three per cent are in low-paid jobs. Only 5.5 per cent have executive positions.

The Ontario Court of Appeal heard a case of pay discrimination in 1970 and ruled that the women involved, nurses' aides working in a Workmen's Compensation Board hospital, "had equal skill, ability and responsibility with the men in doing their job," and should be paid accordingly. The employer who had to stop discriminating against women in that case was the Ontario government.

Ma Bell is not a good mother. Of the 20,000 women who worked for Bell Canada in 1973, only nineteen were in middle management positions, as compared with nine hundred men in middle management, and only one was at an executive level.

In some places the ratio of women in top positions is going

down. In 1970 there were 463 women principals in Ontario schools; four years later there were only 280, and only nine of these were among the six hundred principals of the more prestigious, better-paying high schools.

In 1919-1920, women made up one-quarter of all graduate students in universities across Canada; in 1969, their numbers had dropped to one-fifth. Women make up about a third of enrollment in colleges but they tend to place themselves in such courses as arts and science, education, household science, nursing, and social work (eighty-two per cent of all women college students).

These choices at the university and community college levels accurately reflect how women place themselves in the labour force. They are concentrated in jobs which are logical extensions of traditional housewife chores, such as waitresses, clerks and cleaners. It is probably because these jobs, like child care, nutrition and nursing, are so close to the unpaid work that women normally do in their homes that they are not valued, rewarded, and respected as are the traditional male tasks which have had a dollar value on them ever since currency began.

## You are starting a new job

Newspaper ads are not permitted to classify jobs as MALE or FEMALE so, in theory, you can apply for a job on a construction site or logging operation or flying an Air Canada 747. In practice, however, it is highly unlikely that you have had job experience to qualify you equally with men applicants.

It is interesting to note that many all-male occupations are beginning to discover that women are a good investment. Women truck drivers, for instance, often are more reliable and more considerate of the equipment than some men. If the employer tells you that the work is "too heavy" or whatever, ask him to give you a chance. Very few jobs require a three-hundred-pound weight-lifter, and there are no jobs except modelling jockey shorts which demand a certain kind of genitalia.

When taking a job, arm yourself in advance with the labour regulations which obtain in your province, particularly the prevailing minimum hourly wage. Anyone in a Manpower office should know this or else call the Department of Labour, Women's Bureau, or its equivalent.

If the employer is offering less than the minimum wage, report it. If you permit yourself to be cheated, you are giving consent that others can be cheated.

The law requires that learners be paid, though at a lower scale than regular employees, for a limited length of time. After this period of apprenticeship, the employer must raise your wage to the level of a trained employee. Failure to do so should be reported to the Employment Standards Branch of the Ministry of Labour. (See WHERE TO PROTEST, page 116).

The maximum work week required by law is forty-eight hours, although some union contracts provide a considerably shorter work week. If you work longer than this during a seven-day period, you are entitled to overtime pay, which is sometimes double pay but usually runs to time-and-a-half.

Most provinces limit the amount of overtime you can be required to do, in the interest of your health. In Ontario employees must not work more than one hundred hours a year overtime, but this can vary from province to province. In every part of Canada younger people, usually described as under eighteen, are not permitted to work overtime to the extent allowed adults.

You are entitled to a minimum of four paid statutory holidays: Good Friday, Labour Day, Dominion Day and Christmas Day. Most employees also get New Year's Day, Thanksgiving Day, Victoria Day and Boxing Day, but these are less protected. In most companies you will not be paid for the statutory holiday unless you've been working at the job for a few months immediately previous to it.

It used to be that women could not be required to work after midnight unless a taxi was provided to take them safely home. In the interest of equality many provinces have *dropped* this considerate regulation rather than extending it to men as well.

You may not work longer than five hours at a stretch without an hour off for a meal. Coffee breaks are obligatory in some places, a tolerated habit in others. Wherever large numbers of women are employed, toilet facilities must provide couches, a charming relic of an age that believed women suffer from monthly fits of the vapours. Men, unhappily, are not extended such amenities.

All provinces revise labour legislation on an average of every three or four years so it is impossible to grab such a changeling in these chapters. In general, though, you will receive a bonus of about four per cent of your salary as vacation pay if you leave the job before you have been there a year.

If you stay a year, you get two weeks' vacation with full pay. You are not permitted to take this vacation whenever you please: the time is at the employer's discretion. The longer you stay in the same firm, the longer your vacation will be.

105   You work (for pay)

If you decide to leave, you must give two weeks' notice; if the employer wants to fire you there must be two weeks' notice given to you. In cases where the job has been held a long time, say, between five and ten years, four weeks' notice is required on either side; after ten years of working for the same firm, the period of notice before leaving or firing is eight weeks. Given the tension that often exists at a time of firing or quitting, these regulations often are waived and severance pay of an equivalent amount is substituted.

Sick leave is a company policy, and so is the amount of time permitted to be absent because of the death of a close relative. Check the fringe benefits, such as pension plans and insurance policies. In most cases, benefits are stacked against the families of women employees.

## You work for your husband

This doesn't mean housework. The reason that survey-takers ask brightly, "Do you work or are you a housewife?" is that housework is not regarded as work; neither is working for your husband at his place of business.

Irene Murdoch is Canada's most famous example of this tenet. Though she worked in the fields, mended farm machinery and took care of the animals, alone for five months or more of every year, judges of the land viewed her efforts as part of the marriage contract, no more than was due.

The Federated Women's Institutes of Canada, 55,000 women who are in the main married to farmers, resolved in June 1975, that they would press Ottawa to pass legislation that would permit their husbands to pay them, deduct such payment from their husbands' income taxes, and provide a basis for payment to the women from the Canada Pension Plan.

Women who work on their husbands' farms, clean fish in their husbands' dorries, weigh apples at fruit stores owned by their husbands or keep account books in businesses owned by husbands are usually unpaid, which means they are not covered by sickness, unemployment, vacation or pension benefits other working women enjoy. A main deterrent has been that the husband cannot include such payment as an income tax deduction, as he does for any other person in his employ. And the reason he can't is that the law suspects husbands would use such payments as a fictitious tax dodge, pocket both the wife's wage and the tax benefit and leave the woman no better off than she was before.

Ellen McLean, president of the Federated Women's Institutes, commented "I'm a farmer's wife but my husband can't hire me and deduct the cost. But if he hired the neighbour's wife he can gain tax deductions and make Canada Pension Plan payments."

A survey of working women across Canada was made in the spring of 1975 and investigators discovered that on both coasts families had come spontaneously to the same conclusion: swap wives. Fishermen were hiring their brother's wife or their neighbour's wife, who then hired their wives. It suited government regulations perfectly.

There is concern that matrimonial property laws that require the fifty-fifty split of assets when there is a divorce will work a hardship on couples who have built up small businesses together. It is not likely that either will be able to pay the former spouse one-half the value of the business without selling it, which is detrimental to the interests of both of them. Creative law-makers are at work on alternatives to this undesirable situation.

## Maternity leave

By 1975, six provinces (British Columbia, Saskatchewan, Manitoba, Ontario, New Brunswick, and Nova Scotia) and the federal government through its Canada Labour Code had legislation which prohibited the dismissal of women because of pregnancy and provided maternity leave of seventeen weeks, after which the woman can return to her job without any loss of seniority or scale of pay.

There are some employers, notably airlines, which contend that it isn't advisable from the point of view of maternal or fetal health for women to remain on the job after the fourth or fifth month of pregnancy. Since it is during the first three months that some women feel queasy and spontaneous abortions are most likely to occur, this is a curious line of reasoning. It seems to suggest that the employers are more concerned with the woman's appearance, which begins to alter in the fourth and fifth month of pregnancy, than with her well-being.

Some provinces have the same aversion to the sight of prenatal roundness. Saskatchewan, for instance, hustles pregnant women off the work premises a full twelve weeks before childbirth.

Regulations vary from province to province, but the provisions usually require that the woman be continuously employed for a period of not less than twelve months before she is eligible for maternity leave. This is to prevent, by a comfortable margin, women taking jobs after they discover they are pregnant.

Maternity leave is not paid leave. There are no provisions for pay at all for the first two weeks, but after that, Unemployment Insurance Canada begins to pay benefits which will be maintained for fifteen weeks. To qualify you must have had twenty weeks of insurable employment in the previous year and you must have your doctor sign a UIC medical certificate. UIC will also require proof that you were employed at the time of conception. The doctor is expected to state the date of delivery and UIC counts back nine months. Do not laugh; this is a serious matter.

Because maternity leave legislation was drafted almost entirely by men, it was built around the quaint notion that babies arrive exactly as scheduled, like Swiss trains. Women were expected to commence maternity leave a fixed number of weeks before the anticipated event and were to return to work a certain number of weeks after it, and no sooner.

It turned out to be hilariously unworkable, as any woman could have predicted. Some babies arrive before maternity leave officially begins and some dawdle until the maternity leave has almost expired. Many mothers-to-be would rather work until the last minute so they can spend more time with their newborns, establishing the vital safety-knowledge bond that is the foundation of human emotional health.

The Status of Women Omnibus Bill, an unimpressive piece of minor legislation which was the federal government's response to International Women's Year, provided flexibility in UIC payments for maternity leave. The fifteen-week period of benefits allowed for childbirth are no longer fixed around a mythical delivery date; they can begin with the baby's arrival if the mother prefers. Provincial regulations, however, must be adjusted to be compatible if this is to be effective.

If there is no job for you when your maternity leave has expired, UIC benefits may continue but you must show that your baby does not need you at home and you are therefore free to accept a job. One woman in Toronto was refused UIC payments because, officials claimed, she was breast-feeding her baby and therefore was unemployable. By flourishing a bottle full of formula she was able to establish her claim.

Good infant care is essential to your baby's development if you plan to return to work. It is scarce everywhere in Canada; in fact, it is downright unavailable in most of the country.

Some suggest that maternity leave should be called parental leave and offered to fathers as well, if they choose to care for their infants. A number of men now appreciate the importance and the rewards of helping to launch a new person.

The law says the former job must be waiting at the end of maternity leave, or a job roughly comparable to the former job. Employers, however, often regard a new mother as a poor risk, someone very likely to give up her job and therefore unsuitable for promotion or placing in a training program.

UIC payments do not match job income so maternity leave means less money coming in just as expenses are rising steeply. Women who earn less than $185 a week will find their incomes cut by more than a third during maternity leave.

*The Financial Post* reported that some companies, notably the Bank of Montreal and Bell Canada, share the cost of benefit contributions during maternity leave, which helps a bit. Though it is illegal, a few companies go even further and make up the difference between UIC cheques and the woman's regular salary.

The Canadian Labour Congress in 1974 passed a resolution that women should have full pay and benefits during maternity leave, a suggestion which employers and the government find too expensive to accept. Others protest that it is too expensive for society in the long run not to provide adequately for mothers and their infants; the remedial costs for those who were malnourished or poorly treated in childhood is a budget-breaker at every level of government.

In Cuba, working women who are nursing their babies are permitted time-off from their jobs to do so. Infant care centres are handy, cheap and superbly staffed. Excellent day care is also available, all of it above ground rather than in basements as most Canadian day care is. Cuba, however, has desperate need for women's labour and is willing to provide first rate child care in order to get it. There are even food supplements for pregnant women to protect the health of the baby.

And, finally, in Canada there is no provision for maternity leave or UIC payments when a baby is adopted.

## Income tax

If you are married and living with your husband, your job may cost him money at income tax time. He can claim $1,400 exemption on his tax if you are unpaid or earn less than $300 a year. If you earn between $300 and $1,700 a year, your husband subtracts your total earnings from $1,700 and claims the remainder as his exemption.

You don't have to file an income tax form unless you earn more than $1,978 a year, which is when you stop being a dependent.

You and your husband both file as single people. If there are children, they can be claimed as dependent by whichever spouse has the larger income; the other has no dependents.

Part-time workers, a category in which women predominate, often earn less than the base-line but the employer is required to make income tax deductions at source as though the income was taxable. In that case you make out an income tax form and you will receive those deductions in a refund.

If your husband doesn't work you can claim him as a dependent exactly as men claim non-paid wives.

When you start a new job, it is expected that you may need new clothes or some other items which involve an expense. You can claim three per cent of your income as a "new employment" deduction, up to a limit of $150. No receipts are necessary for this or for medical deductions under $100.

If you are single and the sole support of a relative who lives with you, you can claim exemption of $3,000 a year. If you contribute to an aged relative in order to soften the bleak existence possible on government pensions, the person is not, strictly speaking, dependent on you, and your supplementary contributions are not deductible.

If you have a child, any expenses you incur in caring for that child while you are at work are deductible within limits. You cannot deduct more than two-thirds of your income for the year, even if child care costs you more than that amount. You cannot deduct more than $500 a child, even though that amount is unrealistic so far as day care or baby sitters are concerned. You may not deduct more than a total of $2,000 for your children, which seems to be the Income Tax Department's message that you limit yourself to four children.

When a wife-mother joins the work force her reasons have more to do with economic necessity than personal liberation and enlarging her horizon, since the job she is almost certain to take will be close to drudgery and low-rated. But she does improve the family income. In 1971 it was estimated that there were 1.35 million families in Canada with children under the age of six and the mother out working. The combined incomes in those families came to almost $13,000 a year, as compared to the single income of about $10,000 a year in the 1.8 million families with children under six and the mother at home.

The economic improvement can almost be obliterated when children are small by the cost of child care. The emotional benefits are something else. Some mothers resent bitterly having to spend hours working out of the house, worrying about their children, finding little gratification in the job, and then returning to work even longer hours preparing meals, cleaning the house and caring for the family: a study in the United States in 1973 estimated that a woman who worked a thirty-five-hour week put in another forty hours every week on housework.

On the other hand, some women are exhilarated to be away from homes which tend to isolate them. They gain in confidence, they are building a cushion against the shock of what is called the empty nest syndrome when the children leave home and, to allay one common misapprehension, studies have shown that children of working mothers get into less difficulty with juvenile courts than children of stay-home mothers.

And while there is an impressive body of evidence to prove that toddlers benefit from good day care, it is clear that indifferent, over-worked, understaffed day care facilities are no better for a child than an indifferent, overworked mother— and probably are worse, since the un-friendly place is also strange.

Whether young children are left with a baby-sitter, a relative, a neighbour or day care, it must be a safe, interesting, roomy and varied environment and there must be copious attention paid to the children by dependable, rested, affectionate, knowledgeable adults. Anything less borders perilously on child neglect and abuse.

In 1975 there were 600,000 children in Canada under the age of six whose mothers were in the work force. And yet good day care is rarely an election issue.

## Unions

For the most part, unions in Canada treat women with the same pa-tronizing disinterest that women receive from employers. Some unions are still negotiating agreements which call for lower pay for women who perform tasks shoulder to shoulder with men. Sylva Gelber, direc-tor of the Women's Bureau of the federal Department of Labour, once reminded union leaders that solidarity was supposed to mean everyone in the work force, not just men.

Gelber told a luncheon meeting at the Canadian National Ex-hibition in 1973 that "the average wage rates per hour for men ciga-rette-making machine operators exceeded those of women by 6.7 per cent ten years ago. This differential gap has been increased to 14.4 per cent."

About a half million women are union members in Canada, which represents about one in every six women in the work force. Most union women are concentrated in a few industries, such as public ad-ministration (fifty-four per cent of those union members are women), communications and utilities (forty-two per cent are women), and manufacturing (thirty-seven per cent).

Unhappily, the industries which have the fewest unions are those where working women most commonly are found. Clerks, for instance, are rarely unionized and seventy-two per cent of all clerks are women; it is not co-incidental that the average salary of men clerks exceeds that of women by almost fifty-seven per cent. (Women represent fourteen per cent of managerial occupations, where their average salaries are one hundred and seven per cent lower than those of men.)

Unions, however, help to close the gap between incomes but are as unwilling as management to involve women in the decision-making process. Union leadership is almost an all-male club, just as board rooms are. In 1973 there was only one woman on the twenty-eight member executive board of the Canadian Labour Congress. All ten provincial vice-presidents were men; all ten directors were men; all thirty representatives were men.

CUPE (Canadian Union of Public Employees), a union with thirty-four per cent of its membership women, had only three women on the seventeen-member executive board. United Electrical Workers, with forty per cent of its membership women, had *no* women on the executive board.

The unions which appear to be most active in protecting women from discrimination are CUPE, with a rapidly expanding core of competent women in key positions, the British Columbia Government Employees Union which is powered by woman-energy, the Canadian Airline Flight Attendants Association where the fight against compulsory retirement of pregnant flight attendants is a major issue, and the International Women's Garment Union, which traces its lineage to the sweatshops of the Nineties, where women in their teens died of overwork and poor ventilation.

The executive vice-president of the Canadian Labour Congress in 1975 was Shirley Carr, who indicated in *The Financial Post* series on working women that there was growing pressure on union locals to pay attention to equal-opportunity clauses for women in contract negotiations.

Most of the pressure on management to co-operate comes from public embarrassment in Canada. In the United States, the financial cost of discriminating against women has been an even greater incentive, ever since 1972 when the American Telephone and Telegraph had to pay out about $75 million as the result of a court order obtained by the Equal Employment Opportunity Commission. Since Canada lacks a forceful Bill of Rights, such penalties against employers who discriminate are impossible here.

An example of a union which used its muscle to help women is the Amalgamated Clothing Workers in the Baltimore area of the United States. It put into its contract, and got it accepted, that a network of day care centres would be established at the employers' expense. The employers later admitted that the centres helped their profits.

Another area of negotiated discrimination by most unions is that women are retired earlier than men, at sixty instead of sixty-five, and that they do not begin paying into a pension plan until they have been employed for five years, as compared to one year for men.

In Vancouver some women broke away from their male-led union and tried to work out their grievances from an all-woman splinter group. Such divisiveness probably weakens bargaining positions for everyone. Madelaine Parent, one of the country's outstanding union organizers, recommends that women should become more active in existing unions. If they can't get to union meetings at night because they are doing housework and taking care of their children, they should demand, as the women in the Service, Office and Retail Workers of British Columbia did, that union meetings take place once a month during a two-hour lunch period.

Women should make certain they are represented by women on bargaining committees, where their seniority rights are often given away and there can be indifference to pay disparities.

Women who join unions are probably better protected than women who have no unions, but it is still not true that they are as well defended in their unions as men are.

It puts unions in the solid mainstream of Canadian attitudes towards the work of women, which is to regard it as amateur. Valerie Hunnius of the Office and Professional Employees International Union once reported on a study of 340 Vancouver families with young children where both parents worked. Only thirty-nine per cent of the men helped their wives with the housework on weekdays, only fifty-one per cent on weekends.

## Pensions

Retirement age for women in much of the work force has been sixty, rather than sixty-five which is the normal age for male retirement. This is curious, in view of the fact that women live longer than men do and generally enjoy better health. Since the Canada Pension benefits do not begin until sixty-five for both sexes, many women are left with a five-year scramble for survival.

Pensions, including the government's, have discriminated against the spouses of working women. Even though the women have been paying into the pension plan exactly as men do, payments are not made when she dies except if her mate proves that he is incapacitated and was totally dependent on her. Such a humiliating statement is not required from the widows of men who have paid into pension plans.

Most pensions, except the government's which is geared to age alone, have stopped payment if the widow marries again. They did not stop if a widower marries again.

Amendments made in Ontario in 1975 removed pension plan discrimination because of sex.

## Job training

Community colleges provide job training courses for women returning to the work force after their children are raised. Such education must begin, sadly, with the formidable task of convincing women that they can function successfully in a paid job. Even women who have demonstrated administrative skills in volunteer organizations suffer a failure of nerve when they try to picture themselves as deserving a pay cheque.

Most community college courses for women are one-year snaps, which fit women for traditional low-pay jobs. Longer-term technical courses are mainly filled by men.

It is a reflection of the shaping of women's goals that also happens in high schools, where guidance counsellors think in terms of recognized achievement careers when advising male students, and of support system careers when advising women.

It demands from everyone, men and women, a fresh look at conclusions that society has accepted without reflection for centuries. For instance, when banks were embarrassed by their dismal record of discrimination against women employees, there was an analysis of the cause. It turned out that bank managers almost invariably were men because bank accountants almost invariably were men and it was from this rank of employees that managers are chosen. Banks are now promoting women tellers in increasing numbers to the position of accountant; in 1974 there were 709 of them across the country.

It took an adjustment in attitude, which starts with you. If you are a woman born in the Sixties, you will almost certainly be in the work force for twenty-five years of your life. Do you want to spend twenty-five years at a job below your ability?

# Unemployment

Women are in the category, for the most part, of unskilled labour. They are the reservoir that industrialized nations keep around in case of war or high productivity from some other cause. Because they work more cheaply than men, they are an employer's dream: easy to hire, easy to fire, completely disposable people. They fill the ranks of clerical, cleaning, food industry personnel who are interchangeable components of a company machine.

Despite the belief that women undercut men, unemployment is rising faster among Canadian women. In 1973 it was 5.1 per cent for women employables, a figure slightly lower than that of men (5.9 per cent) but which represented both a steeper rate of increase and a hidden variable, in that women have more of a tendency than men to disappear statistically when they are out of work.

Unemployment Insurance Canada benefits are paid to people who have held a job for not less than twenty weeks during which they contributed a fraction of their pay, matched by their employers, into UIC. Whether you are fired for incompetence or laid off or quit, you cannot collect benefits for two weeks after employment ceases. If you are unemployed because you were fired for misconduct, or because you quit, you must wait six weeks to draw an income.

You must demonstrate that you are actively looking for a job and that you are able and willing to work. One woman in Toronto was cut off because UIC thought she was nursing her baby, thus making herself unavailable for most employment. She had to prove the baby was bottle-fed in order to be reinstated.

The amount you are paid is adjusted in accordance with your previous income. You do not pay into UIC if your income is more than $185 a week (according to the budget of June 1975). People with salaries lower than that receive 66.6 per cent of their previous income.

UIC payments extend for twenty-five weeks after they have begun, during which time there are on-going checkups and reports to be made. If you are still unemployed after that period, benefits may be extended to make a total of no longer than fifty-one weeks altogether.

There is some feeling that women are greater abusers of UIC benefits than men are, that women work a while and nip merrily back into their hammocks and collect the pogey. Like the same charges that are made about welfare recipients, such reports are largely unfounded. If you are tempted to take a government-paid vacation, chances are you'll be caught. More importantly, the person you're stealing from is, in the long run, yourself.

# Where to protest

Women's salaries average almost fifty per cent below those of men. Health and Welfare Minister Marc Lalonde reported that the average income paid to women in 1971 was $4,755 and the average for men was $8,513. Maternity leave is unrealistic, given the unpredictable nature of pregnancies. Pensions and fringe benefits discriminate against women.

There are plenty of pious declarations that women should not be disadvantaged in the work force. The Canadian Bill of Rights (which doesn't work) embodies such concepts fuzzily, but there are provincial amendments to labour legislation which are more specific. Some have teeth in them and sometimes some of them are enforced.

In all cases you can complain on your own behalf or about an injustice to someone else, providing you have her consent. The name of the person complaining is concealed from the employer, though this often is a paper promise: it is likely the employer will guess who did it unless large numbers of employees are involved and there are several other militant women around to confuse possible retaliation.

Your boss is not allowed to fire you or take punitive action because of your complaint, if your identity is exposed. Women have been given unpleasant tasks, however, as a result of a complaint. One woman in a garment factory was given the only place on the assembly line where there were cross-drafts after she complained about her wage disparity.

A third party can lay the claim, providing it is not done anonymously. Typical complaints, according to Judy Stoffman who works for the Women's Bureau in the Ontario Ministry of Labour, are "My niece is working for less than the man next to her on the assembly line" or "I think my wife is getting a raw deal."

Translators are made available as needed for immigrant women, who are among the most seriously short-changed.

A complaint that you lodge to achieve justice for yourself will benefit less articulate, less determined women. When women clerks in one branch of a department store chain were able to prove that men clerks in the same job were better paid, the chain upgraded women's pay across the country. You not only should complain about discrimination, but you have a responsibility to do so; without solidarity, the issue of women's incomes will flop.

You register your grievance with the provincial government labour branch's sword arm. It goes by various names. In Alberta, for instance, the appropriate body is called the Board of Industrial Relations, and in Ontario the Employment Standards Branch. Manpower or the

UIC may be able to direct you. If there is a law school near you, contact the Women's Caucus; telephone a woman lawyer.

If your province has a Human Rights Commission or an ombudsman, make a contact there. Advise your representative in the provincial legislature what you are doing and how it is being handled: you have a lively political issue by the tail. Get in touch with the Women's Bureau of the federal Department of Labour; make certain that your federal Member of Parliament gets a copy of your correspondence.

In short, make a tremendous fuss. Be polite, be patient, but don't give up. Democracy is a machine and, like any other collection of wheels and gears, can rust to death if not used. And the whole fight for women's rights centres on equal pay for work of equal value; women will have won nothing if they do not win that.

## Quebec

Quebec is in a curious state of flux, far ahead of the country in some legislation and back a century in others. It is the only province which in International Women's Year permitted women to be fired because they were pregnant, allowed employers to refuse to hire married women, and accepted union contracts which stipulated that women were to receive as little as half the salaries of men in the same jobs. In Quebec it is permissible for an employer to refuse to promote a woman because of her sex, and to admit it openly.

In the spring of 1975 it was revealed that in the Quebec civil service, three-quarters of women employees earned less than $7,000 a year, while three-quarters of the men employees earned more than $7,000 annually.

# 10 All about welfare

You are eligible for welfare if you are not a minor and if you are destitute. The scant money you receive will confine your diet to high-bulk foods which are heavy in starch and low in protein, which will not be good for your general health; you will wear cheap or second-hand clothes, which will not be helpful to your self-esteem; your mobility will be restricted because of the high cost of transportation, and your outlets for variety and entertainment will be severely limited, which will increase frustration and apathy.

Depending on the supply, you are eligible for subsidized housing, since the cost of housing will otherwise be the most expensive item on your budget and will determine how adequately you can feed yourself and your dependents. Your medical needs will be met, and you are within the guidelines for free legal assistance in most situations. When he was Minister of Justice John Turner once said, "We must understand that the law often contributes to poverty ... for the poor the law appears always to be taking something away."

The National Council of Welfare turned out a report in March 1975, which was called *poor kids*. The opening statement contained this paragraph:

"To be born poor is to face a greater likelihood of ill health —in infancy, in childhood and throughout your adult life. To be born poor is to face a lesser likelihood that you will finish high school; lesser still that you will attain university. To be born poor is to face a greater likelihood that you will be judged a delinquent in adolescence and, if so, a greater likelihood that you will be sent to a 'correctional institution.' To be born poor is to have the deck stacked against you at birth, to find life an uphill struggle ever after. To be born poor is unfair to kids."

There were 812,013 families in Canada living below the poverty line in 1971, according to Statistics Canada. There were 1,729,000 unattached individuals living in poverty; more than half the people over sixty-five years of age in Canada are in that category.

Government supplements, a hodge-podge of allowances and services which are adjusted as the political climate and budget requires, are often criticized as hand-outs which encourage sloth. Every study demonstrates that the overwhelming majority of Canadians who are on welfare are there because they are helpless: more than ninety per cent are old, mentally or physically ill, or are women raising children alone.

The Canadian Civil Liberties Association completed a survey of the abuses against welfare recipients which catalogued the miseries. Its report stated that "Canadian welfare systems are exacting a high price in civil liberties for the provision of subsistence income." It pressures unwed mothers to name and sue their lovers, forces deserted wives to bear witness against their husbands, and by its demand that women who receive welfare must be celibate puts itself in a privacy-invading role of snoop, looking for a man's shirt in the closet or a man's shoes under the bed.

"As long as a recipient hopes to obtain assistance," the report added, "he cannot expect a secure level of freedom from harassment. His dependence on public money may make him subject to periodic investigation and interrogation. For some people this will include a requirement to attend frequently at the welfare office. Such attendance will often be accompanied by long waits in unpleasant surroundings. Few laws or regulations limit the effective power of administrators to intrude upon the freedom of recipients in this way."

Welfare is a trap. Welfare recipients cannot move toward self-sufficiency by testing themselves in a job even part-time because they will lose their welfare support; it is safer to sit at home. Regulations require that the amount of income earned outside of welfare payments must be deducted from the next cheque. It is an administrative headache, arousing suspicion and inquisition in welfare administrators and devious behaviour in the recipients.

People on welfare must give up privacy to a degree that would make other Canadians writhe. They must permit an examination of their assets. They must be almost destitute—and prove it. Their savings must be less than $500 and they must show that no one will help them.

That's humiliating. Also, their premises can be searched without warning. When the recipient is a woman, as it usually is, the inspectors are looking for the "man in the house". Any evidence that a man spent the night under her roof will result in her welfare stopping, since it is assumed he must be paying her for sex.

One Toronto welfare recipient, Ruth Larivière, listed her recommendations for change.

It reads:

"Since our government is spending many dollars to support fatherless families maybe it would be to their advantage to support some kind of program to try and get mothers off welfare and make them want to stay off of it. Here are some ideas.

119   All about welfare

"*Rehabilitation:* Most women on welfare come from low income families or families that have been on welfare themselves. In either situation they don't have very good educations. Therefore they are not able to face a new society, which they would have to face in getting a good job. A program which would teach manners, use of proper grammar, what kind of clothes to wear, personal hygiene. They could gain self confidence from this which would give a lot of incentive in finding a job and holding it. Instead of feeling insecure and changing employment frequently.

"*Education:* Teaching them a form of work suited to their own personality would be next, such as aptitude tests to see what interests them. You can't work at a job you hate. Seeing that they get the course and arranging babysitting service would help remove obstaces also.

"*Loan service:* Women that have been on welfare for any length of time have very limited wardrobes. Maybe a loan service could be arranged so they could buy new clothes. They could have confidence in themselves, their appearance and abilities. The loan would be given those who attended rehab and educational classes reasonably regularly. If they've shown enough interest to go they must be interested in finding and holding a good job. The loans could be repaid after they go to work, such as the university students do who receive them to go to school.

"*Babysitting:* More government operated babysitting services should be available. Some of the mothers wishing to get off welfare could be used. Maybe live-in accommodations could be arranged, such as having various houses around the city for this purpose so women wouldn't have far to travel to drop their children off.

"INFORMING WOMEN OF THIS SERVICE WOULD BE A BIG PART OF THE PROGRAM. IT CAN'T BE OF ANY USE OTHERWISE. WELFARE WORKERS SHOULD BE ADVISED OF THE PROGRAM SO RECIPIENTS WOULD BE AWARE OF IT."

Larivière's reference to child care is crucial to any program to help single-parent welfare recipients. It is estimated that only two per cent of the children of working women have access to day care.

The Canada Assistance Plan, which backs provincial welfare schemes, requires that each province establish appeal boards where citizens who feel themselves ill-handled by welfare officials can state their grievances. Most provinces took their own sweet time before setting up appeal boards—in Ontario the delay was two years—and there has been a marked lack of eagerness everywhere to make sure that welfare recipients know about them.

The "man in the house" rule, however, particularly assaults

the dignity of women and has been a common source of complaint. One Ontario woman, permanently disabled because of cyclamate poisoning and other severe health problems, was denied welfare because a man was living in her house. The welfare review board upheld the decision to cut her off but the case was taken to the Ontario Divisional Court which in March 1975, made a landmark decision that the man in her house could not be labelled a "spouse", which is welfarese for a source of income.

Mr. Justice David Henry called it "an artificial definition". He noted that the two did not share the same last name, property, debts, bedroom or bank account: his presence under her roof and the welfare inspector's assurance that there was a sexual relationship between them did not justify a conclusion that the man was paying her.

"Directors of welfare are frequently clothed with powers to cut off social assistance on the basis of so-called moral judgments," observed Sylva Gelber, Director of the Women's Bureau of the federal Department of Labour. "Although a male resident in her home may not be contributing financially in any way toward the maintenance of the household, the woman is penalized by his very presence."

Deserted wives are particularly vulnerable to the mindless welfare machinery which is geared to the assumption that men should pay for past or present sexual favours. The Anglican Church of Canada once observed, in a study called *The One Parent Family*, that "the public has no idea of the difficulties facing a deserted wife in relation to . . . eligibility for public assistance. Public welfare policy usually requires a woman to lay a charge against her husband in order to establish her eligibility for assistance. For some women the choice is a shocking one: either to testify against her husband or to starve with her children."

Welfare rights groups have been formed everywhere in Canada and most of them have short, stormy careers. The dissension in their ranks reflects the truth that poor people, like rich people, are not a monolith with identical political and tactical views. One of the original ones, Toronto's Just Society, once commented on the unfathomable logic by which governments give mothers desperately meagre allowances to provide for their children, but provide relatively handsomely for foster parents of the Children's Aid Society to care for them.

Until 1970, welfare recipients were unable to receive information on birth control, or any help short of sterilization for spacing or limiting the size of their families. The Family Planning Federation of Canada early that year advised the Senate Committee on Poverty that "the poor in Canada have more children than the non-poor and many of these babies are unwanted." The average number of children for university graduates was then 2.6; for Canadians with no high school education, 3.1; for Canadians without schooling, 4.2.

George Bernard Shaw once called poverty "the worst of dangers, the worst of crimes." He said that "such poverty as we have today in our great cities degrades the poor and infects with its degradation the whole neighbourhood in which they live. And whatever can degrade a neighbourhood can degrade a country, and a continent, and finally the whole civilized world, which is only a large neighbourhood."

## Children of the poor

During the 1971 census it was discovered that Canada has 6.76 million children younger than sixteen years of age. Of that number, 1.66 million were described as poor. The report *poor kids*, prepared by the National Council of Welfare in March 1975, described what that meant—"growing up without as much food as other kids get, without the toys, the clothes and the outings that other kids get."

Almost half the children in Newfoundland grow up below the poverty line. The next saddest part of the country for a child is the Northwest Territories, followed by Saskatchewan and Prince Edward Island, which are almost tied, and Nova Scotia. The proportion of children in poverty is smaller in Ontario and Quebec but because of the size of those provinces they account for sixty per cent of all the destitute children in Canada. Quebec has 529,000 and Ontario 400,000.

Almost all the children (79.3 per cent) live in families where both parents are present; the father is what sociologists call "the working poor". Another 297,000 (17.9 per cent) live with their mothers alone, or some other woman; 46,000 (2.8 per cent) are being raised by a male alone.

When a mother raises her children by herself, the family is almost certain to be poor. Of all the one-parent families in Canada headed by women, seventy per cent are below the poverty line.

Children of the poor suffer from malnutrition, which means they will be smaller than other children, not as healthy, not as able to concentrate, and not as intelligent. A British Child Development Study found that seven-year-olds in poor families were 1.3 inches shorter than seven-year-olds in affluent families. In November 1975 a team of scientists at the University of California reported that "more than a million" North American children suffer brain damage because of early malnutrition.

"It comes as a shock to us," the researchers said. "It implies that a corresponding proportion of the difficulties children experience in school and later in their career development may be due to under-nutrition affecting their brain growth *in utero* and during early life, thus interfering in the most serious way with the quality of their lives and placing an unmeasured but probably significant burden on the rest of society."

There was a shocking study of malnutrition in Canadian children which was conducted in 1971 in schools in Montreal's low-income east end. A health unit examined 3,424 children and found that more than half were physically ill from causes related to malnutrition. Ten per cent, more than three hundred children, were so ill that they were taken to hospitals.

Children of the poor have more difficulty in school than children of the affluent. Along with the handicaps of inadequate nutrition, they suffer from lower expectations. Middle class children aspire to college, lower class children to high school. Children of the poor are more likely to have reading problems and to lack vocabulary range, to be placed in dead-end classes for low achievers, to drop out before they complete high school. And since education is one of the determinants of income, children of the poor are destined to remain poor and pass it on to their children.

They are also more likely to be perceived as delinquents. When a middle class child misbehaves, it is more often seen as a prank, or else, if it is alarming, as maladjustment requiring family counselling or a psychiatrist for the child. Children of the poor are seen promptly by judges when they misbehave. The population of training schools and prisons comes almost entirely from the poor.

The ultimate responsibility for the lives of all Canadian children rests with the government. According to the Criminal Code, when parents fail for any reason to provide the necessities of life to their children, the Crown steps in and takes custody. The government then can be shown to have failed 1.66 million children who live in poverty. There are lawyers who are intrigued by the possibility that a provincial Attorney General or even the country's Prime Minister might be liable for arrest for child neglect. The Canadian government batters babies.

## Fathers on welfare

It merits attention here that men who wish to stay home and raise small children have been denied welfare because they offend welfare's stereotype: men work outside the home, women raise the children. If a mother deserted her children or died, the male parent was expected to hire a baby-sitter.

There is a sound argument on the grounds of the children's emotional health to be made for the father's reassuring and continuous presence after such a crisis. A forty-five-year-old Penetanguishene widower and father of three young children broke the old prejudices in the winter of 1974 when he insisted on his right to receive "Mother's Allowance" support. The Ontario legislature passed a special order-in-council reversing the civil service rulings.

The man concerned told Jean Barfoot, a reporter for the *Toronto Sun*, "I should receive the same consideration as a woman. I should be allowed to raise my family my way ... Most of the administrators in welfare are men and they seem to take the attitude, 'How dare this guy want to be a mother.' They feel it's not manly to want to raise a family."

There are many branches in Canada of single-parent organizations, which include a growing proportion of men. Toronto has a Society of Single Fathers (415-70 Clipper Road, Willowdale, M2J 4E3) which is active in a fight for father's rights. They represent a lot of children. In 1975 there were more than 183,000 children in the country younger than sixteen who were being raised by their fathers alone; 100,000 men are caring for their children by themselves.

# 11 All about credit

Single women have the same relationship to credit as all men do. You can apply for a bank loan or a charge account and expect to either receive it or not on the basis of your income and prospects. Admittedly your income is on the average only half that of men's incomes, and your prospects poorer, but given this disadvantage you are otherwise in the same boat so far as credit is concerned.

The rules change when you marry, and they will never be quite the same again. If you keep your birth name you can minimize your problems but otherwise you disappear. Your credit rating goes into your husband's file at the credit bureau. His credit rating becomes your credit rating, even if you earn the larger income. When you apply for a charge account you may be asked to bring your husband or obtain his signature on the application. (When this happened to Laura Sabia, a lawyer, feminist and first head of the National Action Committee of the Status of Women, she hurled the application back at the credit manager, who promptly decided she could have a charge account without obtaining her husband's permission.)

Partly because of Sabia's indignation, and that of hundreds of other outraged women, major department stores usually refrain from asking for husbands' signatures now. They do persist, however, in making out the card MRS. JOHN DOE. You will have to explain patiently that your name isn't John.

The United States has an Equal Credit Opportunity Act which protects women from discrimination, and some Canadian provinces are moving to make similar reforms, but mainly in Canada it is perfectly legal for a creditor to ask if you are divorced when you apply for credit. One divorced woman earning $20,000 was granted an American Express credit card only when her father signed her application.

Even if you are legally separated from your husband, your credit rating is still tied to his. One solvent independent woman is unable even to rent a television set because her husband doesn't pay his bills.

If you had a credit rating with your bank before your marriage, it probably will drop, whether you change your name or not. Banks justify this by saying that it is a regular part of banking procedure to re-evaluate a client's credit ratings after a change of status. So how come a man's credit rating doesn't drop when he marries?

Banks make it difficult for a married woman to obtain a loan or to cosign a loan for someone else. Wives cannot be held responsible in law for debts they incur on their husbands' behalf, a law which arises from the concept that husbands control their wives and could force them into financial risk situations. Banks therefore routinely ask that a lawyer must be involved when a wife takes out a loan for her husband's business. This is understandable, but managers frequently overstep and ask a woman to consult a lawyer and obtain a lawyer's permission before they will grant a loan for any purpose, or allow her to authorize someone else's loan.

This is nonsense. Complain at once to the president of the bank, or the district manager and/or take your account elsewhere.

One of the consequences of the matrimonial property law reform, giving the non-paid housewife an equal share in the real assets in the event of marriage breakdown, may be that housewives have a recognized credit rating. At present this doesn't happen. If you have been out of the paid work force, you have no credit identity of your own and the dissolution of your marriage will probably put you in a cash-only world. Alimony and maintenance allowances are not considered reliable income by credit-granters.

Credit rating bureaus are required to disclose your credit rating to you, if one exists. If you are married or have been married, it will be filed under his name. You can ask to have it filed separately but people find it harder to change office procedure than their religion and you may have great difficulty.

Toronto has the first Women's Credit Union in Canada, which is set up to provide loans for women starting in business or investing in their own training. Women have great difficulty getting such loans from banks. *Chatelaine* magazine carried a list of horror stories involving women and credit in its August 1975 issue. Written by Ann Berkeley, it included the experience of a regularly employed single woman in her thirties who tried to buy a vacation home and was turned down, despite the cash she had for a down payment; her husband-to-be, a former bankrupt, easily got the loan to buy the same property and had a smaller down payment to offer.

Watch out for credit living. Unless you spend within your means, you will be paying interest charges on late payments that will break your back. There are large holes in consumer protection legislation. For instance, there is a two-to-five-day "cooling off" period on some contracts you sign with a door-to-door salesman: you can cancel the contract if you decide it is beyond your means or something you don't really want. But the same cooling-off is not available if you are pressured into signing a contract in a store, which is a more common setting for sales.

The claims of advertisers are rarely examined in Canada. The truth-in-lending laws which exist in all provinces but Quebec require that you understand what interest is charged on your credit. Since this would shock most purchasers to their marrow, people offering goods on credit do not exert themselves to underline the identifying clauses or interpret what the interest charges mean in terms of dollars.

Most provinces do not regulate finance charges for instalment sales. The Small Loans Act controls the interest on loans below $1,500 but loans above this amount are common when low-income people try to consolidate their debts. There was a recommendation at a Canadian Council on Social Development workshop in Ottawa in 1972 that "the collection of consumer credit debts would be subject to continuous supervision by the courts, and no execution process would issue until after the court had determined the needs of the debtor..."

Meanwhile, beware.

# 12 All about citizenship

You can list yourself as a blank for the purpose of federal elections, rather than "housewife" as was required before the Status of Women Omnibus Bill of 1975. You can also describe yourself as "unemployed" or "not employed" or "retired". "Housewife" is no longer an occupation. It does not seem to most women to be a particularly wonderful reform.

Immigration laws were also changed in the same bill to remove the chattel aspect that used to apply when men were deported from the country. Their wives had to go with them, even if they were Canadian citizens. Dependent members of the family of a deported person can now remain in Canada providing they are over the age of eighteen, or have Canadian citizenship, or have landed immigrant status.

Another overdue reform concerns children born out of the country to women who are Canadian citizens. It has always been in the past that children could take citizenship only from their fathers; the citizenship of the mother didn't count. Now it does.

If you are an Indian woman, you are the most underprivileged person in Canada. You must marry another status Indian or you lose your tribal rights. Indian men may marry white women without jeopardizing their rights or those of their children, but when the reverse happens and an Indian woman mates with a white man, she mysteriously is a non-Indian.

The Supreme Court of Canada narrowly upheld the patriarchal Indian Act in 1973 by a five to four decision. Chief Justice Bora Laskin, dissenting, observed that the status sections of the Indian Act "effect a statutory excommunication of Indian women."

Two years later Mary Two Axe Earley was evicted from her home on the Caughnawaga reserve near Montreal. She was 63 and a widow. It was her childhood home. But she had married a white man.

# 13  All about arrest

Britain and the United States experienced a sharp rise in the Seventies in the proportion of women in the criminal population and a change in the crimes once typical of women from the passive to the violent. Gangs of young women attack, beat up and rob elderly women on the streets of London; Cook County jail for women near Chicago houses a population that is eighty per cent murderers.

Canadian criminologists see signs of this in this country's future but it is still true women criminals here are non-aggressive. Their crimes are shoplifting, prostitution, drug and alcohol addiction, fraud, and child neglect. When they are arrested for some major offense, it is usually because they were the accomplices of men.

Dr. Marilyn Salutin, criminologist with the Centre of Criminology at the University of Toronto, noted, "The typical woman brought into court is there on drug charges (soft and hard), importuning and shoplifting."

More women are being arrested in Canada in recent years, and women are receiving stiffer sentences, but observers believe this is part of a police and court backlash against women's liberation. The tendency born of gallantry to "go easy" on women is no longer prevalent. Still, the woman criminal is rare: for every woman in a federal penitentiary there are seventy men.

In 1975 there was a National Advisory Committee on the Female Offender to examine not only the prisons where women are confined, but the so-called rehabilitation of women in prison. The Commission was told repeatedly that the basic problem of women criminals is a poor self-image, a sense of worthlessness, and that prisons intensify this attitude rather than relieving it. Prisons provide little job training or education upgrading courses for women—in Toronto's Don Jail, for instance, women prisoners make doll clothes—and the sedentary isolation increases the sense of helplessness and worthlessness that predisposed the women to crime in the first place.

The most successful prison rehabilitation program for women is at Purdy in Washington, an estate-like setting where children visit their mothers freely, job and living skills are taught, and women prisoners work in a day care centre where they learn about child development.

The Advisory Committee on the Female Offender heard many recommendations that women prisoners be kept in their own communities rather than be shipped to distant prisons, and that skills leading to self-reliance and self-respect should be taught. The reforms depend on public awareness of the ineffectiveness of a punitive environment to change behaviour, and the acceptance by neighbourhoods of group homes and drop-in programs for ex-offenders.

Canada puts approximately 75,000 people in jail every year. On any given day, one in every one thousand Canadians is serving time, a ratio that is one of the highest in the world. More than eighty per cent of them have committed non-violent crimes. The National Law Reform Commission noted in *Working Paper 11, Imprisonment and Release*, that it costs taxpayers about $14,000 a year to keep someone in prison and concluded that prisons are an expensive and unproductive way of handling the majority of criminals.

"The assumption is that the offender, as a general rule, will return to the community," stated the report. "... In general, the object of facilitating the offender's successful return to the community will be enhanced by permitting living conditions in prison to approximate those in the community."

It suggested that prisoners should be employed for wages comparable with those of other citizens, enabling them to support their families and pay restitution where this is possible, and have an opportunity to participate in recreational, cultural, therapeutic or social programs. Return to the community should be accomplished in stages by enlarging the present Temporary Absence Program which permits daily attendance in school or at a job, with nightly returns to the jail. Commented the National Law Commission, "Such conditions also provide an opportunity for the offender to demonstrate to what extent he is able or willing to resume his responsibilities as a citizen."

## You and the police

You may not be required to answer any question that a police officer asks you except to explain why you are in that particular place at that particular moment. The police have a right to ask you to explain your presence and you must reply. If you are the driver of a car, you are also obliged to produce your driver's license when asked.

Other than when you are driving a car, you do not have to tell the officer your name, your age, your address, your occupation, your political views, your attitude toward drugs, or any information about your friends or family.

It is advisable, however, to behave in a polite manner. An irritated police officer has a number of discretionary alternatives to exercise on uppity citizens, so it is wise to be co-operative. It is not necessary, however, for you to be so co-operative that you climb into the cruiser and cheerily go to headquarters with the officer to talk things over. Unless you are placed under arrest you don't have to go.

There is another myth that police can't enter your premises without a warrant. Royal Canadian Mounted Police have extraordinary powers under what is called a Writ of Assistance which seems to come with the uniform. They can use this tattered document to break down your door and pull your place apart looking for whatever they say they expect to find. If it isn't there they are not too good at apologizing and not good at all at making reparation for whatever damage they cause.

Other police officers can search your home without a warrant if they believe you have weapons on the premises. They do not need a warrant if they intend to arrest someone they believe is there. They can search a car without a warrant.

They cannot otherwise force themselves into your home. You are entitled to refuse entry. If they say they have a warrant, you should ask to see it and check the date and address carefully. Unless you have been arrested, police may not search your person except if there are "reasonable and probable grounds" that you are concealing something illegal.

## Citizen arrest

This is a vigilante style of law enforcement, born of thinly policed frontiers where citizens administered the law themselves, and is much more typical of attitudes in the United States than in Canada, where settlement followed police and church rather than preceding either.

Nonetheless, there is a provision in the Criminal Code for a citizen to make a lawful arrest in certain circumstances, providing the arrested person cooperates by standing still. If you see someone committing an indictable offense you can declare that the person is under arrest and summon a police officer to back you up. An indictable offense is in the range of more serious crimes, such as a theft of goods valued at more than $200. You cannot make a citizen arrest if you see someone shoplifting a pair of gloves. In that situation you are free, of course, to inform a clerk.

You may also make a citizen arrest if you have reasonable grounds to believe someone has committed a criminal offense and is about to escape. An assault, for instance, is a criminal offense.

## You have been arrested

Do not be deluded by television shows from the United States into believing that you have a wide range of rights. In Canada you don't. You have no right to make one telephone call, for instance: that is a courtesy that police officers usually extend but can withhold if they please.

You have a right to remain silent until you have talked with a lawyer, but few policemen will tell you that. You have a right to refuse to sign anything without a lawyer's advice.

The arresting officer does not need a warrant but you must be told what the charge is. Don't offer any resistance from this moment on; it will result in another charge and the police officer is given considerable lattitude in the amount of force that is used to control you.

The chat you have with the police officer over a cup of coffee is never off the record. Neither is your conversation with the friendly policewoman who will accompany you if you use the toilet. Both have a duty to write down what you say and give it as evidence against you in court. Even illegally obtained evidence, such as from an unauthorized wiretap, can be used against you in a Canadian court.

Ask at once for a legal aid lawyer. In some large cities one is available around the clock, but in most places their hours on duty are approximately business hours. Do not discuss your case with the police until you have talked with a lawyer. The law requires that you be brought into court within twenty-four hours of your arrest. You don't plead guilty or innocent at that time. Your appearance is merely to set date of trial and to determine whether or not you can be released from custody until the trial.

The backlash against the Bail Reform Act was packing the jails in the mid-Seventies, but it is still likely that you will be released on your own recognizance without posting any money. If you seem very distraught in the court it can work against you. The judge may decide you need to be detained for a psychiatric examination. If you have failed to show up for trial on previous occasions, or if your crime is a serious one, such as an assault, you may have to post bail or have a financially stable friend guarantee the bail.

You may feel you are guilty of the charge and you want to get it over with by admitting it without bothering to find a lawyer. *Don't*. The consequences of a conviction may wreck your life, to begin with; it is also possible that the charge is unduly heavy and a lesser charge suits your offence better. Young, inexperienced people commonly plead guilty in circumstances that make observers weep for them.

There is a duty counsel present in all courts who is supposed to represent your interests if you do not have a lawyer of your own. Most duty counsels are conscientious people who try to make themselves familiar with the circumstances of each case, but the work load makes this impossible. The duty counsel arrives in court about a half hour before the trials begin and sees the cases on the list for the first time. You and seventeen other lawyerless defendants arrive ten minutes later and sit in the corridor, wringing your hands. In most cases, there is no better than a fifteen-second whispered consultation before your trial starts.

Either get to court early and brief the duty counsel on your predicament or else refuse to enter a plea until you have a lawyer. The judge will remand your case to another date. No fuss. Unless you are in the middle-income bracket, in which circumstances lawyers' fees can break your back, your provincial legal aide will help pay for the lawyer of your choice.

## You are in custody

This is one of the most desolating experiences of a lifetime. A scientist who evaluated the kinds of stress that give people the most pain put being locked in a cell and the death of someone loved at the top of the list of demoralizing events that can happen to a human.

The police wagon is slippery inside. Brace yourself on the turns or you'll be thrown around. At the police station you may be fingerprinted and photographed, side and front. You may be handcuffed and the handcuffs are usually notched to the tightest, which becomes painful.

After you have been booked you are taken to a reception area of the jail. Indication that you are to move is generally given by pushing you. You are fingerprinted again. Your statistics are taken. You are undressed to the skin and there is a search of your vagina and anus. You are given jail clothes, a nightgown, comb, toothbrush and toothpaste, ruled paper, sheets and towels.

It is done impersonally whether you have been arrested many

times before or this is your terrifying, sobbing first time. The authors do not personally know anyone who encountered anyone who was consoling and kind during this ordeal.

Then you are locked up. If you receive permission at your subsequent hearing before a judge, you can be released on bail. If not, you wait until trial date which can be months. In the meantime the jail must produce you once a week in court for a remand.

It won't be much consolation, but prison reform is a continuous and unstoppable fact. Despite such setbacks as the discrediting of bail reform and temporary absence permits, Canadian prisons are improving. In 1843, for instance, prisoners who laughed in Kingston Penitentiary received six lashes.

# 14 Insanity and the law

There's an indistinct line between crime and insanity: some deranged people damage property or other persons because their reason is distorted by illness. In many circumstances the populations of jails and mental hospitals overlap: some people who stroll down a street naked and throw a brick through a window are put in mental hospitals, and others who do the same thing are put in jails.

The choice depends on many factors, not the least of which is the social position of the naked person.

Both criminals and the insane are in the special category of citizens whose freedom can be taken away without their consent. The criminal, however, is much more protected against this happening unfairly than is the person whose behaviour upsets others.

Involuntary commitment to a mental hospital used to be more casual than it is today. Only a few years ago a family could ask any doctor to put Aunt Betty away and if the doctor agreed, the deed was done. Police could diagnose insanity and deliver people to a mental hospital for admission without running into difficulty. Following a series of scandalous revelations that eccentric but sane people were being confined for twenty and thirty years in hospitals, some of them kept there so that others could enjoy their property, the rules began to tighten.

There must now be independent psychiatric examination and assessment. Re-examination must occur on a regular basis when commitment is involuntary and there is an appeal procedure and access to legal aid lawyers in some of the provinces.

It isn't working well enough and large numbers of Canadians are affected. The Law Reform Commission of Canada noted in *Working Paper 14, The Criminal Process and Mental Disorder,* that on any given day in 1974 there were nearly 60,000 Canadians in psychiatric facilities, and several times that number receiving out-patient help for emotional problems. Mental Health/Canada estimates that one in every six Canadians suffers from some form of mental illness during a lifetime and one in every eight will be so incapacitated as to require hospitalization.

Commitment to a mental hospital puts you in a sort of legal limbo. It is not possible for you to enter into a legal marriage, or write a will, or have access to your bank account or credit cards, or buy or sell property, or adopt a child, or vote. You may not be able to get a divorce unless you are in the hospital at least five years. You are in many ways more disadvantaged than someone in prison because it is assumed that your mental state renders you incapable of making reasonable decisions. A Public Trustee will be appointed to administer your business affairs, close up your house, board your dog, or whatever. The Trustee will have to account for all money spent from your accounts.

Shock treatment is still being used in almost every mental hospital or general hospital psychiatric department in Canada. It is highly effective in a certain kind of depression but doctors admit they do not know what it does to the brain and many ex-patients are convinced it is damaging. You cannot refuse treatment if you have been committed involuntarily. Catch 22 operates if you are a voluntary patient and refuse treatment—the staff may decide you are showing signs of serious disturbance requiring that you be made an involuntary patient. Then you get the treatment.

Drug therapy and group therapy are more frequent in mental hospitals. Most have open door policies, so that you can move around, and most look for quick discharge. You may find, in fact, that it is harder to get back into a mental hospital once you have been given a six-week "cure" than it was to get out.

You will probably be able to make telephone calls, unless you make a nuisance of yourself and someone complains, and you can write letters.

The use of legal aid for mental patients is being pioneered in Canada. There has been a long, unresolved debate that confinement in a mental hospital should not occur without the same safeguards to the individual that happen before confinement to a jail, namely, a trial where evidence both pro and con is produced. The manifest problem with this suggestion is that mental illness is not an exact state, and except for a handful of extreme cases the trials would result in doctors testifying on both sides, with one baffled judge in the middle asked to make an impossible decision. The argument goes on.

## Criminal insanity

You cannot be tried for any offense if you are mentally incapable of understanding what is happening. As the Law Reform Commission of

Canada puts it:

"But if the principle is clear, practice is not. Pre-trial diversion of the mentally ill is sporadic and informal. The issue of fitness and legal insanity have been confused in the cases, mixed in psychiatric reports, avoided when they should have been raised, and raised when they should have been avoided.... The result is a strange form of legal double-talk."

When a trial is "postponed" because the accused is said to be insane, this may mean either that the trial will be held later or that the trial will never be held, and the charge, in effect, is dropped. "Acquittal" of someone on the grounds of insanity may mean life imprisonment in a hospital for the criminally mentally ill. Adds the Law Reform Commission, "And all procedures seem to be used interchangeably to achieve the same end—the indeterminate detention of the mentally ill offender."

The first contact the mentally ill person has with the law is with police who have been summoned by someone else. The police officer makes a sidewalk decision whether to arrest the person for whatever offense may have been committed and ignore the signs of derangement, or else to proceed under laws which enable the police to remove anyone "apparently suffering from mental disorder" to a hospital without laying any charge. Police, however, have little or no training in psychiatry and make these decisions as best they can.

Quebec has established a psychiatric assessment centre where Montreal police may take suspected cases of mental illness. In 1974 there were more than a thousand referrals to this centre, of which more than three-quarters were given treatment rather than undergoing arrest. The process is called diversion.

If you are judged to be too ill to stand trial, you become a special kind of ward of the Lieutenant Governor of your province. You will be admitted to a closed mental hospital for treatment until such time as you are judged able to understand and participate in a trial.

The Law Reform Commission observes dryly, "Most of us would rather be found guilty than unfit because the consequences of unfitness are less predictable and potentially more restrictive." Persons unfit for trial must wait for what is called quaintly "the pleasure" of the Lieutenant Governor for release from hospital; in some cases, it never comes. The Commission has recommended that this power be transferred to the trial judge, that treatment never be of indeterminate length, and that persons sentenced for crimes committed under some degree of mental instability must be given treatment, with the right to ask for a transfer to some other hospital if the treatment is not given and a right to transfer to a jail for the completion of sentence, or parole, when the treatment is completed.

Curiously, people who commit violent crimes are among the most readily rehabilitated. At present a number of now-sane people are being confined in prison mental hospitals, apparently forever, because they are legal enigmas.

# 15　You are old

Old is what you make it, and what living made of you. Dr. Harry Maas of the School of Social Work at the University of British Columbia studied old age and discovered that the women who were unhappiest in their declining years were the ones who had centred their lives on their husbands and children completely, together with women who had suffered chronic illness since their youth.

Two kinds of mothers made poor adjustment to old age. Dr. Maas called one group the Fearful Ordering Mothers, "who were submissive, fearful, tending to be depressed," and the other the Anxious Asserting Mothers, "they were more histrionic."

The happiest old women are the ones who had jobs or heavy commitment to volunteer work outside the home most of their lives.

Money is a large factor in the enjoyment of old age. If you have no income beyond the government pension, you will live below the poverty line, which is not conducive to a cheery outlook.

Statistics Canada in 1971 reported that eighty-seven per cent of married women over sixty-five had incomes of less than $2,000 a year; married men were better off: only thirty-six per cent of them were that poor. The average income of married women in the old age bracket was $1,564; the average income of men, however, was $4,346.

When the women were single, divorced or widowed, poverty was slightly more frequent: sixty-nine per cent had incomes below $2,000 a year. The figures for men rose sharply: fifty-seven per cent of single, divorced or widowered men had incomes below $2,000 annually. The average single woman was slightly better off than her married sister, with $2,273 a year; the average single man was worse off than his married brother, at $3,072 a year.

A report, *Sex Discrimination in Fringe Benefits*, prepared for the federal Advisory Council on the Status of Women, revealed that people in Canada get poorer as they get older. Men and women in their seventies were poorer than they had been in their late sixties.

Men are twice as likely as women to have incomes from employment or self-employment after the age of sixty-five; of those who filed income tax forms, forty-three per cent of men were working and only twenty per cent of women. After the age of seventy, the ratio increases sharply: eighteen per cent of income-taxed men are working and only five per cent of women.

After sixty-five, the source of male income is mostly employment, with job pensions second and investment income third. The source of women's income is different: jobs and job pensions are well down the list, which is headed by investment income and the Old Age Pension.

## Pensions

Only thirty-nine per cent of people in the work force are covered by employment pension plans. Women are outnumbered in this group three to one: seventy-four per cent of people covered by company or union pension plans are men and only twenty-six per cent are women. Women make up more than a third of the labour force but are protected by only a quarter of the pension plans, a reflection of the concentration of women in low-coverage industries.

Women in public administration, manufacturing, transportation and communication and finance are as well or better covered than men in those industries but do poorly in community, business and personal service, particularly the hotel and restaurant industries, and when they work in small firms.

Many pension plans set a lower retirement age for women than for men. Of those compulsorily retired at sixty, women outnumbered men three to one.

Pensions are paid to widows of working men for a fixed period that corresponds to the length of service of the employee. They are not lifelong, necessarily; the majority are guaranteed to be not less than five years. If the widow remarries, the pension stops. A number of elderly women accordingly are living in what they would have called when they were young "a state of sin", cohabiting with mates without a marriage ceremony in order to preserve their pension pittance.

Until recently, pension plans were designed for the traditional family of working man and dependent woman. If a woman was working and contributing to a pension plan, her husband could not collect if she died unless he proved he was unemployed and totally dependent on his wife's income. This requirement was not, of course, imposed on widows.

Both the Canada and the Quebec Pension Plan gave leadership

by amending the regulations to cover spouses of working people without any sexual discrimination.

The important element in the Canada Pension Plan is the Guaranteed Income Supplement (GIS) which was added in 1967 to compensate for the rise in living costs. It makes the pension a sort of floating guaranteed annual income which further legislation has reinforced. People over sixty-five receive the Canada Pension Plan monthly payment whether or not they are working or are receiving income from other pensions or investments.

The government's pension plan is the only income most elderly Canadians receive. In 1970 2.8 million people were paying into job pension funds but 8.5 million were contributing to the Canada and Quebec Pension Plans. At that time the average earnings of women contributing to the plans were $3,155; the average earnings of men were $5,945.

Housewives are not covered by either the Canada or Quebec Pension Plan. Since they have no money of their own, they cannot contribute. It is being argued that their contribution is in the form of labour, which should not be disregarded simply because it is free.

Another of the areas where women are disadvantaged so far as pensions are concerned is in requirements for longer periods in the job before pension contributions can commence. This is based on the myth of women turn-over being higher than that of men, and provincial governments are being urged by Status of Women groups to forbid this discrimination.

## Wills

A will can be a simple statement. A farmer, trapped and dying under a tractor, used his own blood to write "All to my wife" and it was upheld in court as a valid legal document.

Most wills, however, are complex and all wills require at some level an acknowledgement of mortality, which is why so few people have drawn one up. If you die without leaving a will, your husband may get one-third of the property and your children two-thirds, depending on the value of your estate and the number of children you have. If you have no children, your husband may get it all.

The line of succession starts with the spouse, followed by legitimate children, followed by parents, followed by the siblings of the deceased, and then nieces and nephews.

You can write a will, in your own handwriting, and sign it. It is called a Holograph Will and requires no witnesses. Another kind of will is called the English Form Will, which you can draw up yourself on a typewriter. You must have two witnesses to your signature and neither of them can be named in the will. The third kind of will is the Notarial Will, in which lawyers usually are involved and the signature is witnessed by a notary. Again witnesses must not be included in the will.

When children are small, it is important for the parents to draw up a joint will covering the possibility that they may be killed together in an accident. The parents designate friends or relatives who will administer their estate on the children's behalf until the children reach the age of majority.

Here are some sample wills. The first includes some of the clauses that might be found in the will of a widow with five children and numerous grandchildren.

THIS IS THE LAST WILL AND TESTAMENT of me, Jane Doe, of the City of Toronto in the County of York, widow.

*Revocation*
1.  I REVOKE all wills and other testamentary dispositions by me at any time heretofore made.

*Trustees*
2.  I APPOINT my daughters Anne, Jennifer and Joan to be the executors and trustees of this my will and I DECLARE that the expression "my trustees" wherever used throughout this my will or any codicil hereto shall mean the executors and trustees or executor and trustee from time to time of this my will.

*Debts*
3.  I DIRECT my trustees to pay out of the capital of my general estate all my just debts, funeral and testamentary expenses as soon as conveniently may be after my death.

*Succession Duties, etc.*
4.  I DIRECT my trustees to pay out of the capital of my general estate as part of the expenses of administration of my estate as if the same were debts of mine incurred by me during my lifetime all succession, estate and inheritance duties and taxes whether imposed by or pursuant to the law of this or any province, state, country or jurisdiction which may be payable by reason of my death in respect of any benefit, gift, devise, bequest, annuity, or legacy given by me during my lifetime or by this my will or by any codicil hereto or in respect of any insurance on my life or any property passing by survivorship or under any power of appointment exercised by me it being my intention that the recipients or beneficiaries of any such benefit gift, devise, bequest, an-

nuity, legacy, insurance or such survivorship or appointed property shall receive the same without deduction of the amount of such succession, estate and inheritance duties or taxes and I EMPOWER my trustees to pay (and to commute and prepay) all such duties or taxes including those relating to interests in expectancy or in remainder within a period of six months after my death or at such later date as they in their absolute discretion shall deem advisable. This direction shall not extend to or include any such duties or taxes that may be payable by a purchaser or transferee in connection with any property transferred to or acquired by such purchaser or transferee upon or after my death pursuant to any agreement with respect to such property.

## Cash Bequests

5. I GIVE AND BEQUEATH
   (a) to my goddaughter        if living at my death the sum of five hundred dollars;
   (b) to my godson        if living at my death the sum of five hundred dollars.

6. I GIVE AND BEQUEATH to each grandchild of mine who is living at my death the sum of one thousand dollars and I authorize my trustees in their absolute discretion to pay any such bequest to a parent or de facto guardian of any grandchild of mine who may be under the age of eighteen years at the time of my death and the recipient of such parent or de facto guardian shall be a full and complete discharge to my trustees for the payment of such bequest.

7. I GIVE AND BEQUEATH
   (a) the sum of five thousand dollars to the Church of        to be used for such purposes as the rector and wardens may determine;
   (b) the sum of five thousand dollars to Dellcrest Children's Centre, Toronto, with the suggestion and request (but without imposing a trust or legal obligation) that it use such sum for its work with pre-school age children;
   (c) the sum of ten thousand dollars to the YWCA, Toronto.

## Bequests of Personal Effects, etc.

8. I GIVE AND BEQUEATH to my three daughters, Anne, Jennifer and Joan, if they are living at the time of my death all my jewellery, personal clothing, furs, trinkets, and other articles of personal use or ornament to be divided between them as they shall agree.

9. I GIVE AND BEQUEATH to my son Fred if he shall survive me all my basic flat silverware in the Kings and Queens designs, including spoons, forks and knives but not including any odd pieces or serving dishes.

10. I GIVE AND BEQUEATH all my furniture and all other articles of domestic or household use or ornament belonging to me at my death, including without limiting the generality of the foregoing

all automobiles, boats, consumable stores, furniture, pictures, books, plate and accessories or equipment wheresoever located to those my children who survive me to be divided among them in approximately equal shares as they shall agree.

### Residuary Estate

11. I GIVE, DEVISE AND BEQUEATH all the remainder of my estate and property both real and personal of whatsoever kind and wheresoever situate including any property over which I may have a general power of appointment (herein sometimes called my "residuary estate") to my trustees upon trust to divide the same into as many equal shares as there are children of mine alive at my death (and I will and declare that if any child of mine shall then be dead but shall have left issue or a spouse then living such deceased child of mine shall be considered as alive for the purpose of such division.)

### Powers to Trustees

13. In addition to all other powers by this my will or any codicil hereto or by any statute or law conferred on them and subject to the other provisions of this my will my trustees shall have power:
    (a) to sell, call in and convert into money the whole or any part of my estate and property both real and personal as shall not consist of money at such time ...
    (b) to retain indefinitely or for such time as they may deem expedient any shares, securities or other investments held by me at the time of my death ...
    (c) to invest and reinvest any moneys at any time and from time to time forming part of my estate in such investments as they may deem expedient notwithstanding that the same may not be legal investments for trust moneys under the laws of the Province of Ontario;
    (d) to mortgage, pledge, exchange or otherwise dispose of any part of my estate as they may deem in the best interest of my estate;
    (e) without the consent of any persons interested under this my will or any codicil hereto to compromise, settle or waive any claim or claims at any time due to or by my estate and to make any agreement with any other person, persons or corporation which shall be binding upon my estate;

    and my trustees shall not be liable for any loss incurred to or in my estate through the bona fide exercise of any of the foregoing powers.

    IN TESTIMONY WHEREOF I have to this my last will and testament written upon this and preceding seven pages scribed my name at Toronto, Ontario, this                day of January, 1976.

SIGNED PUBLISHED AND
DECLARED by the above-
named testatrix, Jane Doe, as
and for her last will and testa-

ment, in the presence of us,
both present at the same time,
who at her request, in her
presence and in the presence
of each other have hereunto
subscribed our names as
witnesses.

This is a sample of a will left by one spouse in favour of the other.

THIS IS THE LAST WILL AND TESTAMENT OF me, Jean Brady, of the City of Toronto in the County of York, of the Province of Ontario, married woman.

*Revocation*
1.  I REVOKE all wills and other testamentary dispositions by me at any time heretofore made.

*Trustees*
2.  I APPOINT MY HUSBAND, Samuel, my daughter, Heather, and the            Trust Company to be the executors and trustees of this my will and I DECLARE that the expression "my trustees" wherever used throughout this my will or any condicil hereto shall mean the executors and trustees or executor and trustee from time to time of this my will.

*Debts, Death Duties, etc.*
3.  I DIRECT my trustees to set aside a fund sufficient to pay:
    (a) all my just debts, funeral and testamentary expenses;
    (b) all pecuniary bequests given by this my will or any codicil hereto; and
    (c) all succession, estate, inheritance and similar duties or taxes whether imposed by or pursuant to the law of this or any other jurisdiction that may be payable in respect to any property passing or deemed by any governing law to pass on my death but excluding any property included or deemed to be included in my estate by reason of the same being acquired on or after my death for inadequate consideration by a purchaser or transferee other than my husband or a child of mine pursuant to an agreement between such purchaser or transferee and myself;
    and to pay all such debts, funeral and testamentary expenses and all such pecuniary bequests and duties and taxes out of such fund. If after all such payments as aforesaid have been made there is any balance remaining in such fund the balance shall be disposed of by my trustees in the same manner as is hereinafter directed for the disposition of my residuary estate.
    I DECLARE that it is my intention that the recipients or beneficiaries of any property in respect of which duties or taxes are payable as aforesaid shall receive the same

145   You are old

without deduction of the amount of any such duties or taxes and I AUTHORIZE my trustees to pay (and to commute and prepay) all such duties and taxes including those relating to life or other income interests or to interests in expectancy or in remainder at such time or times (whether or not overdue) as they in their absolute and uncontrolled discretion may determine.

*Bequests of Personal Effects, etc.*

4.   (a)  I GIVE AND BEQUEATH to my daughter if she is living at the time of my death all my jewellery, personal clothing, furs, trinkets and other articles of personal use or adornment;

      (b)  I GIVE AND BEQUEATH to my husband whatever automobiles and boats I may own at the time of my death, all my furniture and other articles of domestic or household use or ornament belonging to me at my death, including without limitation all consumable stores, books, plate and accessories or equipment wheresoever located if my husband should survive me for ten (10) clear days. PROVIDED THAT my husband shall predecease me or shall not survive me for ten (10) clear days I GIVE AND BEQUEATH all my furniture and all other articles of domestic or household use or ornament as aforesaid to my daughter if she shall survive me.

*Cash Bequests*

6.   I GIVE AND BEQUEATH to my daughter if she should survive me the sum of five thousand dollars ($5,000) for her own use absolutely.

*Residuary Estate*

7.   I GIVE, DEVISE AND BEQUEATH all the rest, residue and remainder of my estate and property both real and personal of whatsoever kind and wheresoever situate including any property over which I may have a general power of appointment (herein sometimes called my "residuary estate") to my trustees upon the following trusts, namely:

      (a)  to invest my residuary estate and pay the net income derived therefrom in quarterly or other convenient instalments to my husband Samuel for and during the remainder of his lifetime;

      (b)  upon the death of the survivor of me and my husband to distribute the capital of my residuary estate to my daughter Heather.

SIGNED etc.

If your will is drawn up by a lawyer, one copy will remain in a safe place designated by the lawyer and you will store another copy in a fire-proof place of your own. At the same time and in the same place, list your insurance policies, the location of your bank accounts, such assets as stocks and bonds, the deeds to any property you own, and a list of the credit cards you hold. You will save someone months of frustration and difficulty thereby.

The lawyer will not disclose the contents of your will to anyone while you are alive, unless you have written instructions to the contrary. Your will remains a protected document even if you are committed to a mental hospital.

The exception to this is when you wish to donate an organ or bones for medical use after your death. You should carry a duplicate of this instruction in your wallet and inform relatives and close friends of your intention. In the event of a sudden death, the signed release will be sufficient to enable your wishes to be carried out with the vital promptness that is required. If you are helpless with a terminal illness, your lawyer is permitted to reveal that aspect of your will to your family and the doctors.

If you wish to donate your body for medical research or education, you can obtain a simple release form from a medical school. Anyone over the age of eighteen can make this decision about her remains. The donor card must be signed by you in the presence of two witnesses. You should carry this card with you at all times and make sure that relatives and friends know about it.

The Department of Anatomy will accept the body and pay for the subsequent burial, providing a brief non-denominational service. If you prefer, the body can be returned to your executor for private funeral arrangements.

If you wish to donate your eyes after death for cornea transplants, you can obtain consent forms from the Eye Bank of Canada through any branch of the Canadian National Institute for the Blind. You are asked to sign the card and show it to your next-of-kin and doctor, and keep it where it can be found quickly.

The courts have ruled that your body belongs to your executor upon your death and not, as many people suppose, to the closest kin. Often these are the same person but sometimes they are not. In the case of large estates, the executor often is a trust company. The executor is not required to carry out your instructions about the disposal of your body. The executor has a free hand to do otherwise.

Your estate pays for the funeral but the executor can be held responsible if the costs are unreasonable.

Gifts or bequests between husbands and wives are not taxable and therefore if your husband leaves everything he owns to you "absolutely and indefeasibily" or you leave everything to him, there is no estate tax when one of you dies. The tax is paid upon the death of the other by your heirs. This obtains in most provinces. Alberta and the Maritimes go further and extract no tax for gifts to anyone. Ontario has no succession duties when one spouse inherits from the other. Alberta and Maritime provinces again have no succession tax at all.

When a property or business is jointly owned, the title passes automatically to the survivor but the property belongs for succession duty purposes to the person who paid for it. The onus of proving which spouse put in the money is on the taxpayer.

If a husband has transferred the family home to his wife, he cannot change his mind upon her death and claim it all back. And vice versa, if you transfer ownership.

All provinces other than British Columbia, Newfoundland, and Saskatchewan provide for your dower right. Alberta, Manitoba, Saskatchewan, and British Columbia have homestead rights. These rights vary from one province to another. For example, Manitoba provides that if the testator doesn't stipulate that his wife can have at least one-third the value of the net estate, she will be entitled to that much anyway.

Dower can be lost by divorce, adultery, or a bar, the latter being the legal term for your decision to give up your dower right. You can bar your dower in a separation agreement, for instance; it is assumed you received some other consideration in exchange for this sacrifice.

If you neglect to make a claim for your dower share of the estate you may forfeit the dower. Some wills contain clauses which stipulate that the widow must accept the benefits named in the will in place of her dower right.

Your husband does not have a dower right to any property you may own. You are permitted, as he is not, to exclude him from any inheritance.

If your husband dies without leaving a will, you can choose between accepting your dower interest in the estate or your interest under your provincial Devolution of Estates Act, which may be more beneficial to you. It depends on the size of the estate.

Your husband can stipulate in his will that your right to the estate ends if you marry again. This is ownership of your vagina from the grave. The benefits, including your dower, then go to the next in line.

If your husband has eliminated you from his will and there is no property over which you can exercise a dower right, you can apply under provincial legislation which covers destitute dependents. In some provinces, common-law wives and children born out of wedlock have been able to secure help under this legislation.

A joint account is a serious mistake if your husband dies. It may be assumed to belong to him, even if you have made all the deposits from your own income. The account will be sealed, together with all bank accounts and safety deposit boxes in the name of the deceased. If you are in need, you may be able to extract money enough for essentials but it is a wise precaution for both spouses to maintain separate bank accounts where contingency funds are kept.

Insurance companies will advance funds if you are in need.

Any will made before a marriage is automatically revoked by the marriage. However, a will drawn up after the engagement, at a time when marriage plans were under way, is considered valid.

You must be eighteen to draw up a valid will in Alberta, Manitoba, Ontario, Prince Edward Island, Quebec, Saskatchewan, nineteen in British Columbia, New Brunswick, Nova Scotia, seventeen in Newfoundland.

Some provinces do not accept the holograph will, the one handwritten and unwitnessed, unless the deceased was a member of the armed service or working on a ship. These include British Columbia, New Brunswick, Nova Scotia, Ontario, Prince Edward Island, and Quebec. Holograph wills are not recommended except as a temporary measure in some perceived emergency.

## You and retirement

If you are a salaried working woman and you don't plan to die young, today is not too soon to plan your retirement. You should know, for instance, that Unemployment Insurance Canada will pay you benefits after you retire, providing you are sixty-five. The Canada Pension Plan also begins payments at sixty-five but the machinery is slow so you will need a cushion. You must apply for the UIC payment—it isn't automatic—and you qualify only if you have had at least twenty weeks of insurable employment in the year preceding your retirement.

Do you have your birth registration? If not, you may have a surprise in store. Many adults of retirement age are discovering that their whimsical fathers registered them under names completely unlike the ones they have been using. The registered name is the legal one and can be adjusted to the more familiar one only through application for Change of Name.

One man found that his father had registered him as Stanley J.J. Freeman and he was in the unique position of being able to pick any two names he liked for himself, providing they began with a J.

Many people find that their parents had imprecise memories of their birth days by as much as a calendar year. They have been celebrating not only the wrong day but the wrong birth year all their lives.

To prepare yourself for retirement, find out exactly what pension plan, insurance policy or other fringe benefit is available where you work. Look at the options available to you and learn how long you must stay in the job to qualify. Check what happens if you should change employers: most fringe benefits are not portable.

Spend a rainy weekend totting up your assets. You need to look at your insurance policies, annuity, pension and retirement savings plans, if any, and find out exactly what your income will be at retirement. If it looks frightfully small, these working years are all the time you will have to do something about it.

The year before you are due to retire, talk to your employer about the benefits and options due you. There are pre-retirement counselling programs and you may be able to line up a part-time or full-time job.

You make your application for your Old Age Security Pension six months before you reach sixty-five.

When you do retire, make certain that you are receiving all the benefits due you. An astounding number of people are so distraught at this time of their lives that they take no initiative on their own behalf. This is no time to cave in: you will need every dime coming to you.

You will have to carry whatever health or medical insurance your employer has been maintaining on your behalf. You need application forms so that bills for the premiums will come to you.

If you have a small bundle of cash, don't make a decision about investing or spending it right away. Sit on it awhile and get the advice of friends who have been in the same boat.

Whether you continue to work or not, you qualify for the Old Age Pension at sixty-five. You need an application for this.

And cheer up. You can travel more cheaply than other people, you can be excused from full taxes on your home, you may receive necessary drugs free, you can get into movies at reduced rates. Your bank may reduce or eliminate certain service charges.

And you'll have time to smell the flowers.

# Appendix:
# Where to go for help

## A. Legal Aid

Free legal aid does not exist in equal accessibility or helpfulness in all the provinces. Ontario has one of the more conservative plans and Quebec one of the best; some provinces have almost nothing.

The following are the names and addresses of provincial directors of established legal aid plans. They may or may not be helpful in your situation.

**Newfoundland:**
Paul R. Stapleton
Administrator
The Legal Aid Committee of the
    Law Society of Newfoundland
287 Duckworth Street
St. John's, Nfld.  A1C 1C9

**Nova Scotia:**
Howard E. Crosby, Q.C.
Executive Director of Legal Aid
Nova Scotia Legal Aid
The Legal Aid Program of the
    Nova Scotia Barristers' Society
2111 Gottingen Street
P.O. Box 1270N
Halifax, N.S.

**New Brunswick:**
E.F. McGinley
Provincial Director
Legal Aid New Brunswick
Barristers' Society of New
    Brunswick
P.O. Box 1144
Fredericton, N.B.

**Prince Edward Island:**
Kenneth R. MacDonald
Secretary-Treasurer
The Law Society of Prince
    Edward Island
Charlottetown, P.E.I.

**Quebec:**
Mr. Justice Robert Sauve
President
or
André Saint-Cyr
Secretary
Legal Services Commission
1170 Beaver Hall Square
Montreal, P.Q.

**Ontario:**
Andrew M. Lawson, O.C.
Provincial Director
Ontario Legal Aid Plan
Suite 1000
145 King Street West
Toronto, Ont.  M5H 3L7

**Manitoba:**
R.J. Meyers, Q.C.
Executive Director
Legal Aid Services Society of
   Manitoba
325 Portage Avenue
Winnipeg, Man.  R3B 2B9

**Saskatchewan:**
Linton J. Smith
Legal Aid Assistance Clinic
   Society
123-20th Street West
Saskatoon, Sask.  S7M 0W7

**British Columbia:**
Frank Maczko
Director
Legal Aid Society of British
   Columbia
2nd Floor
195 Alexander Street
Vancouver, B.C.

**Alberta:**
Legal Aid Society of Alberta
308 McLeod Building
Edmonton, Alta.

**Northwest Territories:**
W. Murray Smith
Director of Public Services
Government of the Northwest
   Territories
Yellowknife, N.W.T.

# B.  Family Planning Aid

**Newfoundland:**
The Family Planning
   Association of Newfoundland
   and Labrador
Medical Arts Building 2
114 Empire Avenue
St. John's, Nfld.  A1C 3G2
   (Branch: Happy Valley,
   Labrador)

**Nova Scotia:**
Planned Parenthood Association
   of Nova Scotia
P.O. Box 7042 N
Halifax, N.S.  B3K 3B4

Metro Area Family Planning
   Association
2172 Gottingen Street
Halifax, N.S.  B3K 3B4

Pictou County Planned
   Parenthood Association
456 Cameron Avenue
New Glasgow, N.S.

**New Brunswick:**
Family Planning Association of
   New Brunswick
86 York Street
Fredericton, N.B.
   (Branches: Edmundston,
   Moncton, Tracadie,
   Campbellton, Northern
   Carleton, Bathurst, St.
   Stephen)

Family Planning Association of
   Fredericton
749 Charlotte Street
Fredericton, N.B.

Family Planning Association of
  Sackville
Box 1195, Medical Centre
110 Lansdowne Street
Sackville, N.B.

Saint John Planned Parenthood
  Clinic Inc.
136 Princess Street
Saint John, N.B.

**Prince Edward Island:**
Prince Edward Island Family
  Planning Association
202 Queen Street
Charlottetown, P.E.I.

**Quebec:**
La Fédération du Québec pour le
  Planning des Naissances
3826 St-Hubert
Montréal, P.Q.
  (Branches: Shawinigan,
  Maniwaki, Hull, Quebec City,
  Rouyn, Mont-Laurier, Gaspé,
  Chicoutimi-Nord, Lac
  Mégantic, Sept-Iles, St-
  Hyacinthe)
Family Planning Association of
  Montreal
336 Sherbrooke Street East
Montreal, P.Q.  H2X 1E6

**Ontario:**
Family Planning Association of
  Hastings and Prince Edward
  Counties
249½ Front Street, 202
Belleville, Ont.

Planned Parenthood Guelph
218 University Centre
University of Guelph
Guelph, Ont.

Planned Parenthood Society
4 Catharine Street North
Hamilton, Ont.  L8R 1H8

K-W Planned Parenthood
35 Scott Street, 105
Kitchener, Ont.  N2H 2P8

Planned Parenthood of London
322 Queens Ave.
London, Ont.

Planned Parenthood Ottawa, Inc.
71 Bank Street, 502
Ottawa, Ont.  K1P 5N2

Birth Control and Family
  Planning Association
165 King Street, 2nd Floor
Peterborough, Ont.

Family Planning Association of
  Niagara
132 Queenston Street
St. Catharines, Ont.  L2R 2Z7
  (Branch: Niagara Falls)

Planned Parenthood of Sarnia-
  Lambton
137 North Christina
Sarnia, Ont.

Family Planning Federation of
  Canada
88 Eglinton Avenue East, 404
Toronto, Ont.  M4P 1B8

Planned Parenthood of Toronto
65 Yorkville Avenue
Toronto, Ont.  M5R 1B7

Planned Parenthood Ontario
Box 3033, Station D
Willowdale, Ont.  M2R 3G5
  (Branch: North Bay)

**Manitoba:**
Family Planning Association of
  Manitoba
304-504 Main Street
Winnipeg, Man.
  (Branch: Brandon)

**Saskatchewan:**
Family Planning Association of
  Saskatchewan
406 Glengarry Block
245-3rd Avenue South
Saskatoon, Sask.
  (Branches: Regina, Prince
  Albert, Saskatoon, Swift
  Current, North Battleford,
  Melfort, Meadow Lake,
  Yorkton)

**Alberta:**
Alberta Family Planning
  Association
204-10711 107th Avenue
Edmonton, Alta.  T5H 0W6

Calgary Birth Control
  Association
223-12th Avenue S.W., 206
Calgary, Alta.  T2R 0G9

Edmonton Family Planning
  Service
616-10136 100 Street
Edmonton, Alta.

**British Columbia:**
Family Planning Association of
  British Columbia
96 East Broadway, 101
Vancouver, B.C.  V5T 1V6
  (Branches: Burnaby, Creston,
  Duncan, Kelowna, Langley,
  New Westminster, North
  Vancouver, Port Alberni, Port

Coquitlam, Surrey,
Vancouver, Victoria, White
Rock)

**Northwest Territories and
Yukon:**
Northwest Territories Planning
  Association
P.O. Box 1680
Yellowknife, N.W.T.  X0E 1H0
  (Branch: Pangnirtung)

Yukon Family Planning
  Association
503 Cook Street
Whitehouse, Yukon

# C. Women's Centres in Canada

**Newfoundland:**
Women's Centre*
P.O. Box 6072
St. John's 753-0220

**Prince Edward Island:**
Women's Travelling Resource
  Centre
285 Kent Street
Charlottetown, P.E.I.

**Nova Scotia:**
Women's Centre (Halifax)*
5683 Brentan Place
Halifax 423-0643
Mailing Address:
P.O. Box 5052
Armdale, N.S.

Women's Centre
P.O. Box 894
Wolfville, N.S.

**New Brunswick:**
c/o Hilary Prince
Y.W.C.A.
Women's Information & Referral
  Centre
27 Wellington Row
St. John

Fredericton Women's Centre
28 Saunders St.
Fredericton, N.B. E3B 1N1

Women's Information Centre
St. John YWCA
27 Wellington Row
St. John, N.B. E2L 3H4

*Has a newsletter.

**Quebec:**
Women's Info. & Referral Centre
3595 St. Urbain
Montreal H2X 2N6
842-4781

La Place des Femmes
3764 Boul. St. Laurent
Montreal 845-7146

**Ontario:**
Women's Centre*
581 O'Connor St.
Ottawa 233-2560

North Bay Women's Centre
2-236 Worthington St. West
North Bay

The Women's Place
968 University Ave. W.
Windsor, Ont.

Women's Place*
25 Dupont St.
Kitchener-Waterloo, Ont.

Guelph Women's Centre
35 Priory St.
P.O. Box 1162
Guelph, Ont.

Women's Resource Centre*
322 Queens Ave.
London, Ont. 432-8693

Women's Resource Centre*
Y.W.C.A.
56 Queen St.
St. Catharines, Ont.

Women's Place
262 Rubidge St.
Peterborough, Ont.

Toronto Women's Bookstore
85 Harbord St.
Toronto, Ont.

Women's Development Centre
15 Birch Ave.
Toronto, Ont. 925-1154

Northern Women's Centre*
c/o Y.W.C.A.
350 Arthur St.
Thunder Bay, Ont.

**Manitoba:**
A Woman's Place
143 Walnut St.
Winnipeg 786-4581

Women's Liberation
c/o Millie Lamb
Ste. 10, 812 Wolseley
Winnipeg

Women's Place
300 Victor St.
Winnipeg

Women's Centre*
Y.W.C.A.
447 Webb Place
Winnipeg, Manitoba

Women's Information Centre
Y.W.C.A.
148 11th St.,
Brandon, Manitoba
727-1130

**Saskatchewan:**
Saskatoon Women's Centre*
124A 2nd Ave. North
Saskatoon

Women's Centre
1 Angus St.
Regina

**Alberta:**
Women's Centre
11812-95 St.
Edmonton

Edmonton Women's Place
9917-116 St.
Edmonton, Alta.

Y.W.C.A. Women's Centre
320 5th Ave.
Calgary

Women's Centre
Old Red Cross Bldg.
Lethbridge

Women's Information Centre
9904-100th St.
Grande Prairie, Alberta

**British Columbia:**
Women's Centre & Bookstore
804 Richards St.
Vancouver 684-0523

Women's Centre
P.O. Box 521
Nelson

Women's Centre
522 Pandora Ave.
Victoria, B.C.

Women's Resource Centre
2961-272nd St.
Aldergrove

Vernon Women's Centre,
Suite 6,
3000-30th St.,
Vernon 545-6552

**North West Territories:**
c/o Nellie Cournoyer
Inuvik

**Yukon:**
Women's Centre*
4051-4th Ave.
Whitehorse

# D. Women's Newspapers

**Prince Edward Island:**
A Woman's Newsletter
Box 1816
Charlottetown

**New Brunswick:**
Equal Times
Cathedral Hall
Church St.
Fredericton, N.B.

**Quebec:**
Québecoises Deboutte
4319 St. Denis
Montreal, P.Q.
$3 per year

Feminist Communication
   Collective
P.O. Box 455
Montreal

**Ontario:**
Status of Women News
121 Avenue Rd.
Toronto
$3 per year

The Other Woman
Box 928 Station Q
Toronto
$2 per year

The Native Sisterhood
P.O. Box 515
Kingston

Tightwire
(Women's Penitentiary
   Newspaper)
Box 515
Kingston
$2 per year

Clearing House for Feminist
   Media
P.O. Box 207
Ancaster, Ont.

Canadian Newsletter of Research
   on Women
Dept. of Sociology
O.I.S.E.
252 Bloor St. West
Toronto, Ont.

The Northern Woman
P.O. Box 314
132 N. Archibald St.
Thunder Bay

Windsor Woman
76 University Ave. W.
Room 603
Windsor

**Manitoba:**
Emergency Librarian
c/o Barbara Clubb
32-351 River Avenue
Winnipeg

**Saskatchewan:**
Network of Saskatchewan
   Women
Box 1525
Rosetown, Sask.

**Alberta:**
Branching Out
Box 4098
Edmonton
$5 per year
$9.50 for 2 yrs.

Source
The Alberta Women's Newsletter
9917-116th St.
Edmonton

Calgary Women's Newspaper
No. 206, 223-12th Ave. S.W.
Calgary, Alta.

**British Columbia:**
Women Can
704 Richards
Vancouver
$3 per year
Kinesis and Western Canadian
    Women's Newservice
2029 West 4th Avenue
Vancouver
Priorities
3485 West 15th Ave.,
Vancouver
$3 per year
B.C. Federation of Women
    Newsletter
1240 Doran Rd.
North Vancouver

**Yukon:**
Victoria Faulkner Newsletter
4051-4th Ave.
Whitehorse, Yukon.

# E. **Regional Contacts**

**British Columbia**
Vancouver Status of Women
2029 W. 4th Avenue,
Vancouver 9

Victoria Status of Women Action
    Group
766 Monterey Ave.
Victoria

Joy Langan
Women's Right Cttee
B.C. Federation of Labour
210-517 E. Broadway
Vancouver

West Kootenay Status of Women
    Council
Selkirk College
Box 1200
Castlegar, B.C.

B.C. Federation of Women
c/o Joy Bradbury
65-445 S.W. Marine Dr.,
Vancouver

Women's Bureau
Christine Waddell
4211 Kingsway
Burnaby

**Alberta**
Alberta Action Committee on the
    Status of Women
M.J. Chorny, President
Provincial Council of Women
3831 Brooklyn Cresc.
Calgary

Jean Marchton, Acting Secretary
9214-117 St.
Edmonton

Calgary Status of Women
Council
223-12th Ave. S.W., Calgary

**Saskatchewan**
Action Committee on Status of
Women
c/o Jane Abramson, Chairperson
2004-14th St. E.
Saskatoon

Gwen Lee, Vice-chairperson
209 St. Andrews Crescent
Box 1525
Rosetown, Sask.

Mary Helen Richards
Corresponding Secretary
1129 Elliot St.
Saskatoon, Sask.

**Manitoba**
Manitoba Committee on the
Status of Women
M. Smith
447 Webb Place
Winnipeg

Manitoba Action Committee
(Brandon)
Women's Information Centre
Y.W.C.A.
Brandon

**Ontario**
Ontario Committee on Status of
Women
Box 188, Station Q
Toronto

Wendy Lawrence
309A-51 Grosvenor St.
Toronto, Ont. M5S 1B5

**Nova Scotia**
Mary Wall
Provincial Council of Women
6851 Regina Terrace
Halifax, N.S.

Muriel Duckworth
Voice of Women—La Voix des
Femmes
6250 South St.
Halifax, N.S.

Judith Wouk
6299 Yale St. Halifax

Dr. Lois Vallely
Dept. of History, Acadia
University
Wolfville, N.S.

**Quebec**
La Fédération des Femmes du
Québec
Pat Buesson
75 12è Ave.
Vimont, P.Q.

Centre de Renseignements, F.F.Q.
45 rue est Jarry
Montreal

**Northwest Territories**
NWT Status of Women Action
Committee
Alison J. McAteer, Co-ordinator
P.O. Box 1225
Yellowknife X0E 1H0

Ellen Binder
P.O. Box 1057, Inuvik, N.W.T.

**New Brunswick**
Marjorie Laws
Business and Professional
Women's Club
595 Shediac Road, Moncton, N.B.

Janet Culinan
Human Rights Commission
P.O. Box 6000
Fredericton, N.B.

Hilary Prince (YWCA)
27 Wellington Row
St. John, N.B.

Norah Toole
824 George St.
Fredericton, N.B.

**Prince Edward Island**
Status of Women Action
    Committee
Martha Practt, Acting Secretary
57 Newland Cres.
Charlottetown, P.E.I.

P.E.I. Council of Women
c/o Beatrice Reeves
R.R. 1
Charlottetown

**Newfoundland**
Newfoundland Status of Women
    Council
Wendy Williams, President
Celia Griffith, Treasurer
Box 6072
St. John's

**Yukon Territory**
Yukon Status of Women Council
4051-4th Ave.
Whitehorse

**National Action Committee on
the Status of Women**
Lorna Marsden, President
419 Markham Street, Toronto

Grace Hartman, Immediate Past
    President

233, rue Gilmour, Suite 800
Ottawa

Laura Sabia, Past President
29 Edgedale Road
St. Catharines, Ontario

Cathleen Morrison, Secretary
184 Moore Avenue
Toronto

Moira Armour, Editor
Status of Women News
121 Avenue Road
Toronto, Ont. M5R 2G3

Marjorie Robertson
Typesetter, Toronto

# Glossary of Legal Terms

**Abstract of Record**  complete history in short abbreviated form of the case, as found in the record

**Abstract of Title**  chronological history in abbreviated form of the ownership of a parcel of land

**Action in Personam**  action against the person, founded on a personal liability

**Action in Rem**  action for the recovery of a specific object, usually an item of personal property such as an automobile

**Allegation**  assertion, declaration, or statement of a party to an action, made in a pleading, setting out what she expects to prove

**Amicus Curiae**  friend of the court, not being a party in the cause, who interposes with the permission of the court and volunteers information of law or fact of which the court can take judicial notice

**Appellant**  party appealing a decision or judgment which she considers unfavourable to a higher court

**Appellate Court**  court having jurisdiction of appeal and review; not a **trial court**

**Arraignment**  in criminal practice, the formal reading of a charge to an accused person in open court

**At Issue**  Whenever the parties to a suit come to a point in the pleadings which is affirmed on one side and denied on the other, they are said to be *at issue* and ready for trial, and written pleadings are closed.

**Bail**  to set at liberty a person arrested or imprisoned, with or without security being taken, for her appearance on a specified day and place to answer criminal charge

**Bail Bond**  obligation signed by the accused, with or without sureties, to secure her presence in court

**Bind over**  to hold on bail for trial

**Brief**  written or printed document prepared by counsel to file in court, usually setting forth both facts and law in support of the case; also the act of instructing counsel in the preparation of a case for presentation

**Burden of Proof** in the law of evidence, the necessity or duty of affirmatively proving a fact or facts in dispute

**Cause** suit, litigation, or action, civil or criminal

**Certiorari** original writ commanding judges or officers of inferior courts to certify or return records of proceedings in a cause for judicial review

**Change of Venue** removal of a suit begun in one county or district to another, for trial, or from one court to another in the same county district

**Circumstantial Evidence** evidence of indirect nature, from which the fact is not directly proved but may be inferred

**Codicil** supplement or addition to a will

**Commit** to send a person to prison, asylum, workhouse, or reformatory by lawful authority; or to commit to trial after preliminary hearing

**Common Law** law which derives its authority solely from usages and customs of immemorial antiquity, or from the judgments and decrees of courts; also called *case law* as distinct from *statute law*

**Commutation** change of punishment from a greater to a lesser degree, as from death to life imprisonment

**Competency** in the law of evidence, the presence of those characteristics which render a witness legally fit and qualified to give testimony

**Complainant** synonymous with *plaintiff*

**Concurrent Sentence** sentences for more than one crime in which the time of each is to be served concurrently, rather than consecutively

**Consecutive Sentence** separate sentences (each additional to the others) imposed against a person convicted upon an indictment containing several counts, each charging a different offence, one sentence to begin at the expiration of another

**Contempt of Court** any act calculated to embarrass, hinder, or obstruct a court in the administration of justice, or calculated to lessen its authority or dignity (Contempts are of two kinds: *direct* and *indirect*. Direct contempts are those committed in the immediate presence of the court; indirect is the term chiefly used with reference to the failure or refusal to obey a lawful order.)

**Contract** oral or written agreement between two or more parties which is enforceable by law

**Corpus Delicti** facts which constitute an offence

**Corroborating Evidence** evidence supplementary to that already given and tending to strengthen or confirm it

**Costs**   allowance for expenses in prosecuting or defending a suit (Ordinarily this does not include full legal fees of recipient.)

**Counterclaim**   claim presented by a defendant in opposition to the claim of a plaintiff

**Courts of Record**   those whose proceedings are permanently recorded, and which have the power to fine or imprison for contempt (Courts not of record are those of lesser authority whose proceedings are not permanently recorded.)

**Criminal Insanity**   lack of mental capacity to do or abstain from doing a particular act; inability to distinguish right from wrong

**Crown**   Sovereign in right of Canada or a province; used also in referring to the rights, duties and prerogatives belonging to the Sovereign; also used frequently in referring to the lawyer representing the Sovereign in litigation

**Damages**   pecuniary compensation which may be recovered in the courts by any person who has suffered loss, detriment, or injury to his person, property or rights, through the unlawful act or negligence of another

**Decree**   decision or order of the court (A *final decree* is one which fully and finally disposes of the litigation; an *interlocutory decree* is a provisional or preliminary decree which is not final.)

**Default**   A *default* in an action at law occurs when a defendant omits to plead within the time allowed or fails to appear at the trial.

**Direct Evidence**   proof of facts by witnesses who saw acts done or heard words spoken, as distinguished from *circumstantial evidence* which is called *indirect*

**Direct Examination**   first interrogation of a witness by the party on whose behalf she is called

**Directed Verdict**   instruction by the judge to the jury to return a specific verdict

**Dismissal Without Prejudice**   permits the complainant to sue again on the same cause of action, while *dismissal with prejudice* bars the right to bring or maintain an action on the same claim or cause

**Domicile**   that place where a person has his true and permanent home

A person may have several residences, but only one domicile at a time.

**Double Jeopardy**   common-law prohibition against more than one prosecution for the same crime, transaction, or omission

**Embezzlement**   fraudulent appropriation by a person to his own use or benefit of property or money entrusted to him by another

163   Glossary of Legal Terms

**Entrapment**   act of officers or agents of a government in inducing a person to commit a crime not contemplated by him, for the purpose of instituting a criminal prosecution against him

**Escheat**   right of the state to an estate to which no one is able to make a valid claim

**Escrow**   a writing or deed, delivered by the grantor into the hands of a third person, to be held by the latter until the happening of a contingency or performance of a condition

**Estoppel**   person's own act, or acceptance of facts, which preclude her later making claims to the contrary

**Exclusion of Witnesses**   order of the court requiring all witnesses to remain outside the courtroom until each is called to testify, except the plaintiff or defendant

**Ex Contractu**   In both civil and common law, rights and causes of action are divided into two classes: those arising *ex contractu* (from a contract) and those arising *ex delicto* (from a wrong or tort).

**Ex Post Facto**   after the fact; an act of fact occurring after some previous act or fact, and relating thereto

**Executor**   person named by the deceased in her will to carry out the provisions of that will

**False Arrest**   any unlawful physical restraint of another's liberty, whether in prison or elsewhere

**False Pretenses**   designed misrepresentation, with a view to defraud, of existing fact or condition whereby a person obtains another's money or goods

**Fiduciary**   term derived from the Roman law, meaning a person holding the character of a trustee, in respect to the trust and confidence involved in it and the scrupulous good faith and candor which it requires

**Garnishment**   proceeding whereby property, money, or credits of a debtor in possession of another (the garnishee) are applied to the debts of the debtor

**Garnishee**   person upon whom a garnishment is served, usually a debtor of the defendant in the action; to institute garnishment proceedings

**General Assignment**   voluntary transfer by a debtor of all her property to a trustee for the benefit of all of her creditors

**Guardian Ad Litem**   person appointed by a court to defend an action or other proceeding on behalf of an infant or mental incompetent

**Holographic Will**   testamentary instrument entirely written, dated, and signed by the testator in her own handwriting

**Hostile Witness**   witness who is subject to cross-examination by the party who called her to testify, because of her evident antagonism toward the party as exhibited in her direct examination.

**Implied Contract**   contract in which the promise made by the obligor is not expressed, but inferred by her conduct or implied in law

**In Camera**   A trial or other proceeding is said to take place *in camera* when it is heard privately, the public being altogether excluded.

**Indeterminate Sentence**   indefinite sentence of "not less than" and "not more than" so many years, the exact term to be served being afterwards determined by parole authorities within the minimum and maximum limits set by the court or by statute

**Indictment**   accusation in writing found and presented by a grand jury, charging that a person therein named has done some act or is guilty of some omission which, by law, is a crime

**Intestate**   one who dies without leaving a will

**Leading Question**   one which instructs a witness how to answer or puts into her mouth words to be echoed back; one which suggests to the witness the answer desired; prohibited on direct examination

**Libel**   defamation expressed by print, writing, pictures or signs; in its most general sense, any publication that is injurious to the reputation of another

**Limitation**   a certain time allowed by statute in which litigation must be brought

**Lis Pendents**   pending suit

**Locus Delicti**   place of the offense

**Malfeasance**   evil doing, ill conduct; the commission of some act which is positively prohibited by law

**Mandate**   judicial command or precept proceeding from a court or judicial officer, directing the proper officer to enforce a judgment, sentence, or decree

**Manslaughter**   unlawful killing of another without malice; may be either voluntary, upon a sudden impulse, or involuntary, in the commission of some unlawful act

**Master**   officer of the court, usually a lawyer, appointed for the purpose of dealing with matters preliminary to trial; used most frequently in interlocutory applications concerning pleadings and conduct of the action before trial

**Material Evidence**   such as is relevant and goes to the substantial issues in dispute

**Mistrial**   erroneous or invalid trial; a trial which cannot stand in law because of lack of jurisdiction, wrong drawing of jurors, or disregard of some other fundamental requisite

**Mitigating Circumstance** one which does not constitute a justification or excuse of an offense, but which may be considered as reducing the degree of moral culpability

**Moral Turpitude** conduct contrary to honesty, modesty, or good morals

**Municipal Courts** in the judicial organization of some jurisdictions, courts whose territorial authority is confined to the city or community

**Murder** culpable homicide where the person who causes the death of a human being means to cause his death or means to cause him bodily harm that he knows is likely to cause his death, and is reckless whether death ensues or not

**Negligence** omission to do something which a reasonable person, guided by ordinary considerations, would do; or the doing of something which a reasonable and prudent person would not do

**Next Friend** adult representing the interests of an infant or a mentally incompetent person who is the plaintiff in a legal proceeding; which adult becomes a party to the action

**Nisi Prius** courts for the initial trial of issues of fact, as distinguished from appellate courts

**Nolle Prosequi** formal entry upon the record by the plaintiff in a civil suit, or the prosecuting officer in a criminal case, by which he declares that he "will no further prosecute" the case

**Non Compos Mentis** not sound of mind

**Out of Court** One who has no legal status in court is said to be *out of court*, i.e., he is not before the court. For example, when a plaintiff, by some act of omission or commission, shows that he is unable to maintain his action, he is frequently said to have put himself out of court.

**Plaintiff** person who brings an action; the party who complains or sues in a personal action and is so named, on the record

**Pleading** process by which the parties in a suit or action alternately present written statements of their contentions, each responsive to that which precedes and each serving to narrow the field of controversy, until there evolves a single point, affirmed on one side and denied on the other, called *the issue*, upon which they then go to trial

**Power of Attorney** instrument authorizing another to act as one's agent or attorney

**Preliminary Hearing** synonymous with *preliminary exam-*

*ination*; the hearing given a person charged with crime by a magistrate or judge to determine whether he should be held for trial

**Preponderance of Evidence**   greater weight of evidence, or evidence which is more credible and convincing to the mind, not necessarily the greater number of witnesses

**Probate**   act or process of proving a will to be actually that of a deceased

**Probation**   in modern criminal administration, allowing a person convicted of some minor offense (particularly juvenile offenders) to go at large, under a suspension of sentence, during good behavior, and generally under the supervision or guardianship of a probation officer

**Quid Pro Quo**   something for something; old term for consideration

**Removal, Order of**   order by a court directing the transfer of a cause to another court

**Rest**   A party is said to *rest* or *rest her case* when she has presented all the evidence she intends to offer.

**Retainer**   act of the client in employing her lawyer or counsel; also denotes the fee which the client pays when she retains the lawyer to act for her and not against her

**Rule of Court**   order made by a court having competent jurisdiction

Rules of court are either general or special: the former are the regulations by which the practice of the court is governed; the latter are special order made in particular cases.

**Search Warrant**   order in writing, issued by a justice or magistrate, directing an officer to search a specified house or other premises for stolen property; usually required as a condition precedent to a legal search and seizure

**Self-defense**   protection of one's person or property against some injury attempted by another

The law of *self-defense* justifies an act done in the reasonable belief of immediate danger. When acting in justifiable self-defense, a person may not be punished criminally nor held responsible for civil damages.

**Separate Maintenance**   allowance granted to a wife for support of herself and children while she is living apart from her husband but not divorced from him

**Slander**   base and defamatory spoken words tending to prejudice another in his reputation, business or means of livelihood

*Libel* and *slander* both are methods of defamation, the former being expressed by print, writings, pictures or signs; the latter orally.

**Stare Decisis**   the doctrine that, when a court has once laid down a principle of law as applicable to a certain set of facts, it will adhere to that principle and apply it to future cases where the facts are substantially the same

**Statute**   written law as created by a legislative or other body empowered to pass law in contradistinction to the unwritten law arising out of custom and adopted by the courts

**Subpoena**   process to cause a witness to appear and give testimony before a court or magistrate

**Summons**   writ directing the sheriff or other officer to notify the named person that an action has been commenced against her in court and that she is required to appear, on the day named, and answer the complaint in such action

**Tort**   injury or wrong committed, either with or without force, to the person or property of another

**Transcript**   official record of proceedings in a trial or hearing

**Undue Influence**   whatever destroys free will and causes a person to do something she would not do if left to herself

**Unlawful Detainer**   detention of real estate without the consent of the owner or other person entitled to its possession

**Usury**   taking of more for the use of money than the law allows

**Venue**   particular county, city or geographical area in which a court with jurisdiction may hear and determine a case

**Voir Dire**   trial within a trial to determine the admissibility of evidence before its submission to the jury or tribunal

**Warrant of Arrest**   writ issued by a magistrate, justice, or other competent authority, to a sheriff or other officer, requiring her to arrest the person therein named and bring her before the magistrate or court to answer to a specified charge

**With Prejudice**   The term, as applied to judgment of dismissal, is as conclusive of rights of parties as if action had been prosecuted to final adjudication adverse to the plaintiff.

**Without Prejudice**   A dismissal *without prejudice* allows a new suit to be brought on the same cause of action.

**Writ**   order issuing from a court requiring the performance of a specified act, or giving authority and commission to have it done

2 3 4 5 6 WO 80 79 78 77 76